Interviews with Ali Pacha

Peter Oluf Brøndsted

INTERVIEWS WITH ALI PACHA OF JOANINA

in the autumn of 1812;
with some particulars of Epirus,
and the Albanians of the present day

Edited with an introduction by
Jacob Isager

THE DANISH INSTITUTE AT ATHENS
1999

ISBN 87 7288 840 7

Distributed by
AARHUS UNIVERSITY PRESS
University of Aarhus
DK-8000 Aarhus C
Fax (0045) 86 19 84 33

79 Lime Walk
Headington
Oxford OX3 7AD
Fax (0044) 1865 750 079

100 Main St.
Box 511
Oakville, Connecticut 06779
Fax (001) 860 945 9468

Cover: Ali Pasha of Ioannina hunting on the Lake of Butrinto in March 1819. From L. Dupré: *Voyages à Athènes et à Constantinople ou Collection de Portraits, de Vues et de costumes Grecs et Ottomans*, Paris, 1825, Pl. VIII.

Plate 1 (facing the title page): Peter Oluf Brøndsted. Oil painting by C.A. Jensen. Ny Carlsberg Glyptotek, Copenhagen.

Acknowledgments

I wish to express my gratitude to Ida Haugsted for her assistance and Thomas Basbøll for revising my English.

Professor V. Panayotopoulos, the Centre for Neo-Hellenic Research at the National Hellenic Research Foundation, kindly accepted to read Brøndsted's manuscript and I want to thank him for his collaboration and the great interest he has shown in this project.

The illustrations are provided by the courtesy of the Gennadius Library, Athens, the Bibliothèque Nationale et Universitaire de Strasbourg, the Royal Library, Copenhagen and the Ny Carlsberg Glyptotek, Copenhagen.

I wish in particular to thank the Eleni Nakou Foundation and the Ny Carlsberg Foundation for their economic support for the printing.

Athens, November 1998   *Jacob Isager*

Contents

Preface

An early promoter of cultural relations between Denmark and Greece was the Danish scholar Peter Oluf Brøndsted, who travelled in Greece in the years 1810-1813. He was considered a pioneer in the field of archaeology and became famous on the publication of his excavations on the Island of Kea and of his investigations of the Parthenon marbles.

Six additional volumes on ancient and modern Greece were planned. After Brøndsted's sudden death in 1842, his manuscripts from a series of well attended lectures on his travels were published in Danish. They may give an idea of what the six volumes were intended to contain.

The present book is the first publication of a manuscript which Brøndsted certainly wanted to present to readers outside Denmark, namely his "Interviews with Ali Pacha of Ioannina in the year 1812" — published here for the first time. The year 1812 was a fateful one in the history of Europe. Brøndsted's text was written after the death of Ali Pasha in 1822 and reflects the period in which that revolution started which finally resulted in the independence of Greece. It presents its author as a person well versed in politics, with mind open to foreign customs and manners, greatly, but far from uncritically, fascinated by Ali Pasha of Ioannina.

The Danish Institute at Athens welcomes the opportunity to publish this entertaining and thought-provoking Danish contribution to the political and cultural history of Greece.

The Danish Institute at Athens
November 1998

Signe Isager
director

I have a variety of acquaintance, French, Danes, Germans, Greeks, Italians, and Turkish, and have contracted an alliance with Dr. Bronstedt of Copenhagen a pretty philosopher as you'd wish to see...

(Byron in a letter to Francis Hodgson, dated Athens, January 20th, 1811)

I am at present out of spirits having just lost a particular friend; poor dear Dr. Bronstedt of Copenhagen (who lost half his rixdollars by our cursed bombardment) is lately gone to Constantinople; we used to tipple punch and talk politics...

(Byron in a letter to John Cam Hobhouse, dated Athens, March 5th, 1811)

Introduction

In the letters quoted on the previous page, Lord Byron declares his friendship for the Danish archaeologist and philologist Peter Oluf Brøndsted, characterizing him as a pretty philosopher, who liked to tipple punch and talk politics. This is, in fact, a very accurate description of the man, who in this pamphlet — entitled "Interviews with Ali Pacha of Ioannina" — presents himself as a keen observer of the ways in which power can be used and abused in the hands of a despot, and, at the same time, openly declares how much he enjoys the company of the same Ali, who revealed himself as a most courteous and entertaining host to visitors.

Brøndsted is at once fascinated and repelled by Ali, who, born an Albanian, succeeded first in establishing himself as a head of the ever rivalling clans of Albania and later became Turkish governor of the greater portion of Northern Greece, while one of his sons, Vely, ruled the Morea. In apparent accord with the Sultan in Istanbul, Ali ruled his pashalic for a long time as if it were his own kingdom and demonstrated his independence in politics as well as in the administration of his subjects. Brøndsted openly admires the way in which Ali has brought unity to Northern Greece and he remarks more than once that it is safer to travel in Ali's states than in most other countries of southern Europe. The only robber you meet is Ali himself, Brøndsted concludes, leading him to the following generalization:

A single privileged plunderer is better than a multitude of subaltern tyrants, not only for travellers, but also for the inhabitants of any country whatever; at least some arrangements can be made with one only, but there is no stipulating with a host of petty plunderers; besides despotism, though in its nature monstrous and sterile, still occasionally produces something good, whilst anarchy, the pest of all social order, never brings forth anything profitable whatsoever.

I refer the reader to the pamphlet itself for Brøndsted's further reflections on ways of solving the problem of Balkanization. It is the addition of such reflections, that gives this pamphlet its special value compared to the edition of Brøndsted's *Reise i Grækenland i Aarene 1810-13* (Travels in Greece in the years 1810-1813), in two volumes — an edition of his manuscripts from a series of well-attended lectures, given in Copenhagen between 1815 and 1817. It was published only in 1844, two years after Brøndsted's death. Like the pamphlet, this edition (vol. I, 236-70) gives a vivid description of his stay in Prevesa, his meetings with Ali Pasha, and his visit to the ruins of Nicopolis with Ali. And although the "Interviews" often simply repeat the content of the Danish text, they supply, being written much later, the political and philosophical considerations of a more mature Brøndsted, considerations which could now be seen in the light of the Greek struggle for independence and an awakening consciousness, in Denmark and elsewhere in Europe, of the need for new constitutions.

Thus, the main reason behind Brøndsted's decision to publish his "Interviews with Ali Pacha" separately and to make them available to an international public in an English, as well as a German and a French edition, was without doubt to present the extraordinary and contradictory person of Ali Pasha as an important political figure in Southeastern Europe with an enormous influence all over Greece.

In his correspondence Brøndsted reflects on Ali Pasha as the instigator of a Greek uprising against the Sultan and thereby on his role as a catalyst for the Greek war of independence. A letter written in Paris May 11th 1824 to Mrs Kamma Rahbek, who held a central position in the Danish *societé littéraire*, exemplifies the same two-sided personality which Byron describes: the political philosopher and the connoisseur of the good things in life.

Enclosed you will find a little cane around which are wrapped two pages. I ask you to accept it as a new remembrance of an absent, faithful friend. One of the pages shows a young, innocent, by heavenly harmony inspired angel, the young Liszt, created by the Lord in his mercy, as an inspiration and refreshment for many a noble heart. The other depicts an old man, a genius, but at the same time a callous devil, created by the Lord in his wrath as a scourge for degenerate races: Ali Pacha of Ioannina. The last mentioned has had his day.

The Lord broke his heart of stone, when its destiny was fulfilled which was to arouse the dormant Hellas from its long-lasting lethargy...

Brøndsted does not tell us more about Ali in this letter, but being a skilled pianist himself, he expands on Liszt's renown as a *Wunderkind* in the *salons* of Paris. Liszt and Ali make a strange couple, but the comparison clearly shows that Ali Pasha has made an lasting impression on Brøndsted, which, eventually, after Ali's dramatic death in 1822 by order from the Sultan, led him to the idea of making his conversations with Ali known to the world.

P.O. Brøndsted and Greece

There is no need to provide a biography of Ali Pasha in this introduction, since Brøndsted gives us a detailed account of Ali's life in the pamphlet. I will, therefore, confine myself to the task of providing an outline of Brøndsted's extraordinary career as a scholar, his investigations and excavations in Greece, his years in Rome as a royal Danish envoy at the Holy See, his residence in Paris and London, and his activities in Copenhagen as professor of philology and archaeology until his death.

Brøndsted was born in 1780 as son of a vicar. But, as his close friend and biographer J.P. Mynster remarks, despite his provincial upbringing, his behaviour was by no means maladroit nor rustic. Before he reached the age of 16 he was sedate and neat in appearance, and moved with ease in all social circles. He was of good health and of a strong constitution from which he later benefitted when traveling, often under very primitive conditions.

As a young man, he was a great admirer of Napoleon and no friend of the English; later he completely changed his mind about them both.

In 1802 he graduated with a degree in theology from the University of Copenhagen, took up studies in philology and was awarded the gold medal in 1804. At the same time he took active part in the social life of the town. He was fond of music and a competent piano player. He was engaged to Frederikke Koës, whom he soon after had to leave for seven years. She was 15 years old and the sister of his close friend,

2. Georg Koës, engraved by Andreas Flint, Paris 1808.
The Royal Library, Copenhagen.

the philologist Georg Koës. In 1806 Koës and Brøndsted, now *Dr.Phi-los.*, set out to fulfill Brøndsted's boyhood dream of visiting Greece. Koës was financed by his family whereas Brøndsted was supported by the Fund *ad usos publicos*.

Travelling through Germany they were delayed by the battle of Jena; and in Weimar they took part in Goethe's wedding festivities. In Dresden, the Danish poet Adam Oehlenschläger joined them en route for Paris, where they spent more than three years examining collections and libraries in preparation for Greece. In the summer of 1809 they left

Paris heading for Rome, which in the same year had been occupied by the French. Here they met three persons who would become their close friends and members of their entourage in Greece: the German architect Carl Haller von Hallerstein from Nürnberg, the German landscape painter Jacob Linckh from Württemberg and Baron Otto Magnus von Stackelberg from Estonia. Together they planned their expedition to Greece. To avoid difficulties with the Turkish authorities the two Danes were to act as Danish envoys to the Sublime Porte (Constantinople) and Haller to act as their Secretary, while Stackelberg and Linckh joined them as common travellers.

Their primary goal was to provide a description of Greece, ancient and modern, its topography, history, arts and customs. In this way they followed the well known pattern for "Travels in Greece...", but Koës' studies in Greek music, which unfortunately were never published, would have constituted an addition to the genre. Stackelberg and Haller also seem to have been connoisseurs of music. A proper, common plan for their work was made only after they had spent two years in Greece — the stay in Greece was originally planned to last eight months.

In a letter written April 9th, 1812 in Athens, Brøndsted outlines to Haller, Linckh and Stackelberg — Koës had died the year before — their plan for a description of Greece based on scholarly observation and excavations, in which the members of the group contributed with *cahiers*, written by one or more authors according to their interest and special knowledge. No efforts were to be spared in the presentation of the texts and the illustrations. Cotta in Tübingen is suggested as publisher. The letter, which gives many details of their plan, is quoted in the exhibition catalogue *Carl Haller von Hallerstein in Griechenland 1810-1817, Architekt, Zeichner, Bauforscher*, Berlin 1986, 22-23. Haller's early death in 1817 left his work unfinished, and only Brøndsted and Stackelberg remained as contributors to the series.

The expedition left Rome in May, 1810, stayed in Naples for a while, and after having suffered a shipwreck they finally reached Corfu in late July, 1810. An illness forced them to remain at Corfu for almost a month, but on August 25th, they reached Prevesa, where they got their first impression of a Turkish city. Two days later they were able to visit their first ruins on Greek soil, the ruins of Nicopolis, the City of Victory, founded by Augustus after the battle of nearby Actium in 31 BC.

3. Carl Haller von Hallerstein. Drawn by Otto Magnus von Stackelberg on Zakynthos, 1814. München, Staatliche Antikensammlungen.

Haller's drawings from the ruins are dated August 28th, the day they left for Patras.

The party arrived in Athens on September 14th and its members soon felt themselves at home. They got acquainted with Lord Byron, who in a letter (to Francis Hodgson), dated November 14th, 1810 makes the following remarks about the travel companions:

I have kicked an Athenian postmaster, I have a friendship with the French consul and an Italian painter, and am on good terms with five Teutones and Cimbri, Danes and Germans, who are travelling for an Academy. Vale.

The French consul was the artist Louis Fauvel, and the Italian painter Lord Elgin's agent Giovanni Battista Lusieri. Brøndsted's extant Greek diaries relate the period from August 24th, 1810 to February 8th, 1811. He mentions that he met Byron a couple of times, and that he, on New Year's Eve 1810, discussed with him, among other things, the triple alliance between Russia, England, and the Porte. In another diary note from the 13th of December he describes Byron's face as pretty and noble and his appearance as magnificent (quoted in Ida Haugsted, *Dream and Reality, Danish antiquaries, architects and artists in Greece*, London 1996, p. 19 with note 26).

During the winter they made investigations in Athens and surroundings. Here they also met with the English architects Charles Robert Cockerell and John Foster, who joined their group and contributed with plans and ideas.

As Byron notes, Brøndsted left Athens in early spring 1811 for Constantinople and the western coast of Asia Minor, accompanied by Koës and Stackelberg, while Haller, Linckh, Cockerell and Foster started their succesful excavations of the Temple of Athena at Aegina. About the first of August, Haller and Linckh went to the island of Zante (Zakynthos), accompanied by Koës who had returned to Athens before his companions. Here Koës died of pneumonia, only 29 years old. Brøndsted, who had to interrupt his journey in Asia Minor because of a heavy attack of dysentery, got the news of his friend's death on his way back to Athens. He confided his thoughts to his diary, five hours from Athens by foot, on a beautiful October evening with clear transparent air and a stunning view across the sea to Aegina and the Argolid:

It feels for me, as I draw closer to Athens, as though I was approaching my Fatherland. I will enjoy this happy feeling, while I can. I am not yet inside the walls of Athens. Inside await letters and tidings of my only friend's departure from me and from my dearest. I came with him from Korinth to Athens thirteen months ago, in an altogether different mood...

In the winter of 1811-12 Brøndsted made excavations on the island of Kea, which among other things resulted in his correct identification of the ancient cities on the island. Later in the spring of 1812 we find him working at Aegina and Salamis and in June he joins Haller in his excavations of the temple of Apollo near Phigalia (Bassae). From Arcadia he proceeds to Laconia, where he is attacked and robbed on the heights of the Taygetus shortly before he reaches Kalamata. He later tells Ali Pasha of the troubles it caused him. In September, he begins his journey back to Denmark, visiting the tomb of his friend Koës on Zante on the way, and obtains the details of his death from countess Maria Lunzi, the widow of the Danish consul at Zante, who had taken care of Koës in the last days of his life. Her son Nicolo, then 15 years old, followed Brøndsted to Denmark and became very fond of the country. He remained there until 1819, finding his second home in the house of Brøndsted.

After stops on Cephalonia and Ithaca, Brøndsted reaches Prevesa on December 12th, 1812 and meets with Ali Pasha, who may have been as interested as Brøndsted in discussing political matters at this crucial point in the history of Europe, where the troops of Napoleon had reached Moscow and begun their retreat in the Russian winter. Surely this was a topic to be debated in the seraglio of Prevesa. Brøndsted does not tell us about this explicitly, but he relates, in the introductory part of the pamphlet, how Ali — as a consequence of the French Expedition to Egypt and the hostilities of the Sublime Porte against France — late in 1798 succesfully attacked the French garrison in Prevesa and subsequently sent their heads to Constantinople. Referring to some Greeks in Ioannina as his sources, Brøndsted relates that after Napoleon's victories in Italy, Ali was tempted to change policy in favour of France against the Turks, but thought better of it and remained hostile to France, which seems to have particularly annoyed the Emperor Napoleon.

Ali's flirtations with the French found strange expressions such as his confiscation of several boxes of exquisite Greek vases which were made ready for shipment to England by Lord Elgin's agent Lusieri. They were instead presented by Ali to the Emperor Napoleon. It may have been instigated by the artist Fauvel, the French consul in Athens. Brøndsted states, that he would have liked Lusieri "had he not demolished the splendid Parthenon", and he calls the incident "a lovely Story" in his diary for September 23th 1810 (quoted by Haugsted, *Dream and Reality*, p. 19 and note 28. On Lusieri: note 29).

The pamphlet tells the story of Brøndsted's conversations with Ali Pasha and his opinion of the man and shall not be repeated here.

4. Peter Oluf Brøndsted. Charcoal drawing by Henrik Plötz, 1813. The Royal Library, Copenhagen.

Brøndsted spends January and half of February 1813 in Ioannina, the capital of Ali's pashalic. From Corfu he sets out for Italy, stays in Rome for five weeks and after stops in Florence, Venice, Vienna and in several German cities he reaches Denmark in September, 1813.

Here he was appointed *professor extraordinarius* in philology; and in the lectures mentioned earlier (above, p.12), he made a preliminary presentation of the material collected in Greece. He married Frederikke Koës who she gave birth to a son and two daughters over the following four years. Frederikke died a few days after the birth of her youngest daughter and in this unhappy situation Brøndsted decided to leave his infant children in the care of his wife's twin sister and her husband and return to Rome to carry on with the work which he felt was the mission of his life: to publish the results of his investigations in Greece. In Athens an agreement had been made among the companions to meet again in Rome — an ideal place, not far from Greece — for the final researches and preparations for the publication of their results.

He leaves Denmark in September 1818. In Weimar he visits Goethe, who asks him to stay an additional day for further discussion of a topic of common interest: Greek art. He confides to his diary: "How happy I was to see the old eagle again. He still grumbles, as usual; he is 12 years older now, but no less stout, yet he has lost some of his mobility". In Nürnberg he meets Haller's brother, from whom he gets the news of Carl Haller's death in the valley of Tempe, where he had been hired by Vely Pasha, the son of Ali, to construct a bridge.

The good company of his many friends in Munich made him stay there until the New Year. In late January 1819, he finally reached Rome, where he had secured for himself a position as Royal Danish envoy at the Holy See, for which he got a yearly allowance. He soon found out that here, like in Copenhagen, the daily routine took up much of his time. Brøndsted took great care in introducing contrymen to the city, and he helped the Crown Prince of Denmark, Christian Frederik, a personal friend of Brøndsted's, to purchase antiquities. In Rome, as in Munich, his many friends, among which were Stackelberg, Linckh and the Danish sculptor Bertel Thorvaldsen, helped him to accept the loss of his wife and his separation from his children. In the month of May he revisited the Ionian islands in order to bring back the young count Lunzi to his mother at Zante.

His outspokenness combined with his declared sympathy for the revolution in Naples in 1820 made him unfit for his position as ambassador and, eventually, after a *démarche* from Vienna, he was relieved of his allowance. One main reason for this was a comment that he made in the preface of a dissertation on the inscription of a bronze helmet, printed in Naples in 1820. He had expressed what a manifestation of vanity it would be to assume that a few words from a stranger as himself about a piece of art should arouse the interest of many, when this stranger happened to stay in a country, where the magnanimous prince finally had bestowed on his people the most precious gift that can ever be given to mortals: freedom.

In a reply to the Danish Minister, who critized his opinion as not being in agreement with his government, Brøndsted uttered his astonishment that the government expected to get from him what they wanted to hear, whereas he assumed that it was his duty to report what actually happened. He made no secret of the fact that he found the revolutionary tendences in many countries, especially in Greece, a sincere expression of the wishes of an oppressed people, not the machinations of some secret societies or conjurations.

Brøndsted stayed in Rome at his own expense and maintained his good relations with Denmark. In his correspondence with Prince Christian Frederik, he writes about his concern for the revolt in Greece and relates accounts related to him from his friends in Greece.

In 1823, he had to go to Paris to supervise the last preparations for the first part of his "Voyages dans la Grèce accompagnées de recherches archéologiques". He stopped at Geneva, where he had made arrangements for a linguistic revision of the French manuscript. There he much enjoyed the company of count Kapodistrias, with whom he could share his affection for Greece and its fight for freedom.

The book came out in 1825 and was followed by a German edition. It contained a description of the ancient cities on the island of Kea, their geography, history and historical monuments, with emphasis on his excavations of the ancient Karthaia. The book was profusely illustrated with prints.

The following years are spent in Copenhagen, London, and Paris, and Brøndsted is able to devote most of his time to the preparations of the next volume.

The revolution in Paris 1830 was of great interest for Brøndsted. "This revolution seems until now in every respect to be the most dignified and the most beautiful we have witnessed; this time, at least, all law and order was on the side of the people, while injustice and violence were on the side of its adversaries", he remarks in his diary for August 7th.

About this time the second volume of his Voyages were published. In the preface, Brøndsted announces his joy of the victory over the Turks at Navarino (1827). This volume was dedicated to his friends Thorvaldsen and Cockerell, "dignes disciples et heureux imitateurs de Phidias et d'Ictinus". The theme of this volume was "The Parthenon on the Acropolis of Athens, in an archaeological and historical context". His investigations of the metopes on the south side of the building constituted an important part of it. His first volume was well received, and the new volume contributed further to his European fame. We know from a recital of Brøndsted's works, held by W.R. Hamilton in the Royal Society of Literature 1843 in memory of Brøndsted, that a manuscript with studies of the pediment groups of the Parthenon existed at that time. But it was never printed, and with the second volume the series — which was to have consisted of eight volumes — stopped. A dissertation on "Panathenaic vases" was printed in the *Transactions* of the Society in 1832 (French translation 1833).

In 1832 Brøndsted, now 52 years old, returned to Denmark. He was appointed *professor ordinarius* in philology and archaology and at the same time accepted a position as director of the Royal Collection of Coins and Medals. He took great interest in this collection and provided casts of the *desiderata* in the collection from London and Paris. He felt much honoured when, in 1836, he became a member of the Society of Dilettanti in London, which the same year published his treatise on "Bronzes from Siris" (two relief embellished fragments of a suit of armour, from the 4th century BC, found near the river Siris in Lucania). Brøndsted published a German edition in Copenhagen the following year.

At the age of 61, he fell from his horse during a ride and his strong constitution unfortunately allowed him to walk to the nearest hospital where he was diagnosed to have suffered no external injuries. He died soon after from injuries to his internal organs.

Following the ancient biographical tradition, Brøndsted's biographer Mynster gives us a description of the man: Of short stature, but strong and muscular, with a face that was not beautiful, but often enlivened by the interest and the love that animated him. He preferred elegance to splendour. He surrounded himself with furniture that was both comfortable and of high quality workmanship. This, combined with his collection of exquisite objects of art, made it a real pleasure to visit him.

He had an extraordinary memory and apart from his knowledge of the ancient languages — Greek, Latin, and Hebrew — he mastered with great ease German, French, English, Italian, and Modern Greek, spoken and written, as well as some Spanish and Turkish.

Brøndsted describes in a letter his own intellect in this way:

My feelings never deceive me, but my intellect is rather slow and of an often obstinate indistinctness, which, eventually, disappears, when I industriously endeavour to develop what I long ago felt had to be the case. That is why ... I normally have a far better understanding of Pindar and Aeschylus than of Thucydides and Demosthenes. The former I understand immediately and by instinct, whereas I often have to read the latter again and again, even where every single word already is known to me...

Brøndsted was, in fact, an excellent philologist and, among other things, produced a fine translation of the *Oresteia*. But it was as an archaeologist that he made his main contributions to the study of the ancient world. He was a pioneer in this field — *"facile princeps* in the department of Archaeology", as Hamilton proclaimed him in his memorial speech in the Royal Society of Literature.

In the article on Brøndsted in the Danish encyclopedia, *Salmonsens Konversationsleksikon*, vol. IV (1916), we find this conclusive evaluation:

Judging from Brøndsted's rich talents and his education, his efforts could have been of higher aims. He found it difficult to dwell on a topic for a longer period. Good company, music, sports, and things of general interests engaged his attention very much. But what he produced was characterized by painstaking preparations, a brilliant mind and a clear presentation.

Byron was less moralizing. He did not even mention Brøndsted's qualifications as a philologist or archaeologist. In his description, Brøndsted is presented as an entertaining cosmopolite with great knowledge in many fields. As the above-mentioned Mynster expresses it:

He was by nature a communicative person and he had something to say. He had visited, and often lived for a longer period, in most of the larger and more remarkable cities in Europe; he had known and often stayed with not only most part of the famous scholars and artists, but many political notables and remarkable people of all kinds...

Surely, Ali Pasha is to be included in this last group.

The Manuscript and the Illustrations

The manuscript of Peter Oluf Brøndsted's "Interviews with Ali Pacha of Ioannina in the autumn of 1812" can be found in the Royal Library of Copenhagen together with a German and a French version, all collected in the same folder (KB NKS 341c fol.). Fair copies have been made of the English and the French version. All the translations seem to have been made by the author himself. They are not dated, but the text refers to the death of Ali Pasha, which means that it has been composed after 1822.

In the text Brøndsted has used the letters of the alphabet to number his notes. Those letters are kept in this edition together with numerals indicating notes. Notes indicated with numerals only are the editor's notes. Brøndsted's spelling of names and titles such as "pacha" and "Joanina" are kept in his text, whereas "pasha" and "Ioannina" are used in the introduction. Comments of the editor are put in square brackets.

Brøndsted has prepared illustrations for his text and refers to them in his notes and mentions that some plates have been made, but unfortunately they are not preserved. The information given in the notes has made it possible to recreate some of material that Brøndsted wanted to use.

The other illustrations used in this edition are, with a few exceptions, drawings made by Brøndsted's companions, Carl Haller von Hallerstein, Otto Magnus von Stackelberg, and C.R. Cockerell.

List of Illustrations

Cover illustration: Ali Pacha de Janina chassant sur le lac de Butrinto en Mars 1819. From L. Dupré: *Voyages à Athènes et à Constantinople ou Collection de Portraits, de Vues et de costumes Grecs et Ottomans*, Paris, 1825, Pl. VIII.

dessin exécutés sur les lieux en 1811 par le Baron O.M. de Stackelberg et publiés à Rome 1825. No 9.

Pl. 10, p. 41. Soldato Albanese. From: *Costumes et Usages des Peuples de la Grèce Moderne* gravés d'apres les dessin exécutés sur les lieux en 1811 par le Baron O.M. de Stackelberg et publiés à Rome 1825, No. 31 (This plate is reproduced from a special edition with 40 plates; the other edition from 1825 has only 25 plates).

Pl. 11, p. 45. Ismaël Bey et Mehemet Pacha. Fils de Veli, Pacha de Thessalie, et Petit-fils d'Ali Tebelen, Visir de Janina. From Dupré, *Voyages...*, Pl. IV.

Pl. 12, p. 53. Carl Haller von Hallerstein: Seraglio di Ali Pascha apresso Nicopolis. Nicopoli, seraglio dell "Ali Pascha", 1810, 28. Aug. 19 x 25.1 cm, Bibliothèque Nationale et Universitaire de Strasbourg (BNUS), Ms 2724², 5; Bankel (see Plate 3) No. 1073.

Pl. 13, p. 56. Giannizzaro di Ianina. Stackelberg, *Costumes...*, No. 1.

Pl. 14, p. 57. Uffiziale Albanese. Stackelberg, *Costumes...*, No. 17.

Pl. 15, p. 61. Ali Tebelen, Pacha de Janina dessiné d'apres nature le Mars sur le lac de Butrinto, 1819, from Dupré, *Voyages...*, Pl. VII).

Pl. 16-17, pp. 68-69. Carl Haller von Hallerstein: Nicopolis heut zu tage Paleocastro, Nicopolis = Paleocastro, 1810, 28. Aug. Two sheets, each 19 x 25.1 cm, BNUS, Ms. 2724², 5; Bankel nos. 1874 and 1875.

Pl. 18, pp. 72-73. Carl Haller von Hallerstein: Nikopolis. "Vorgebirge von Actium" — Insel Sa. Maura. Zurückzeite des grossen Theaters von Nikopolis. 1810. 28. Aug. 19.7 x 49.8 cm., BNUS, Ms. 2724², 5; Bankel No. 1876.

Pl. 19, p. 76. Le Palais et la Forteresse de Janina, vue du lac. Un Turc et un jeune Grec. From Dupré: *Voyages...*, Pl. IX.

Pl. 20, p. 78. Carl Haller von Hallerstein: Morceau de Mur du ci-dessous nommé Paleo Kastro appellé ajourd'hui εις το ριζαμ [?]. Paleo Castro = Nicopolis, 1810, 28. Aug. 14.5 x 18.5 cm., BNUS, Ms. 2724², 5; Bankel No. 1877.

Pl. 21, p. 80. Carl Haller von Hallerstein: Autre part du mur. O. Terrasses du ci-dessous Paleo Castro [top]. Plan de la terrasse [bottom]. Paleo Castro = Nicopolis. 1810, 28 Aug. 14,5 x 18,5 cm., BNUS, Ms. 2724², 5, Bankel No. 1878).

Bibliography

Angelomatis-Tsougarakis, H., *The Eve of the Greek Revival. British Travel-lers' perception of Early Nineteenth-Century Greece*, London 1990.

Aravantinos, S.P., Ἱστορία ᾽Αλῆ Πασῆ τοῦ Τεπενλῆ συγγραφεῖσα ἐπὶ τῇ βάσει ἀνεκδότου ἔργου τοῦ Παναγιώτου ᾽Αραβαντινοῦ, Athens 1895.

Bankel, Hansgeorg (Herausg.), *Carl Haller von Hallerstein in Griechenland 1810-1817. Architekt, Zeichner, Bauforscher*. Im Auftrag der Carl Haller von Hallerstein Gesellschaft. Berlin, 1986.

Bartholdy, J.L.S., *Bruchstücke zur nähern Kenntnis des heutigen Griechen-lands, gesammelt auf einer Reise im Jahre 1803-1804*, Berlin, 1805.

(Beauchamp, Alphonse de), *The life of Ali Pacha of Jannina, late Vezier of Epirus surnamed aslan, or the Lion*. Second ed. London, 1823, printed for Lipton Relfe. (The book contains no information of its author).

Beresford, G. de la Poer, *Twelve Sketches in Double-tinted Lithography of Scenes in Southern Albania* by Captain G. de la Poer Beresford., London, 1855.

Brøndsted, P.O., *Sopra un'iscrizione Graca scolpita in un antico elmo di Bronzo rinvenuto nelle ruine di Olympia del Peloponneso con alcune notizie sopra l'isola d'Itaca*. Lettera del Cavaliere D. Bröndsted dell' Università di Copenaghen, agente della reale corte di Danimarca presso la Santa Sede. Napoli, 1820. (English version in *Classical Jour-nal*, vol. XXIX, No. LVII: A Letter on a Greek Inscription engraved on an Ancient Helmet of Brass, discovered in the Ruins of Olympia in the Peloponnesos, which Helmet has been most graciously accepted by His Majesty, from Maj. Gen. Sir Patrick Ross, K.M.K.J. and placed in the British Museum: also some observations on the Island of Ithaca, by ...

—, *Voyages dans la Grèce accompagnés de recherches archéologiques, et suiv-is d'un apercu sur toutes les enterprises scientifiques qui ont lieu en Grèce depuis Pausanias jusqu'à nos jours*, I-II, Paris, 1826-30.

(German edition: *Reisen und Untersuchungen in Griechenland nebst Darstellung und Erklärung vieler neuentdeckten Denkmälern griechischen Styls, und einer kritischen Übersicht aller Unternehmungen dieser Art von Pausanias bis auf unsere Zeiten*, I-II, Paris 1826-30).

—, *A brief description of thirty-two ancient Greek painted vases, lately found in excavations at Vulci, in the Roman territory, by Mr. Campanari, and now exhibited by him in London...* , London, 1832.

—, *On Panathenaic vases, and the holy oil contained in them...* Letter addressed to W.R. Hamilton, Esq. From the Transactions of the Royal Society of Literature, vol. II, part I, p. 102-35, London, 1832.

—, *The bronzes of Siris, now in the British Museum.* An archaeological essay by P.O. Bröndsted. London, 1836.

—, *P.O. Brøndsteds Reise i Grækenland i Aarene 1810-1816*, I-II. Tillige indeholdende Forfatterens Biographie ved J.P. Mynster. Udgivet af N.V. Dorph. Copenhagen 1844. (Includes a biography in Danish pp. 2-86 and a bibliography pp. 87-92).

—, *Uddrag af reisedagbøger.* Udgivet af N.V. Dorph, Copenhagen 1850.

—, *The excavation of the temple at Phigalia after P.O. Broensted's unpublished manuscript* by M. Hammerich. Copenhagen, 1861.

—, *Breve fra P.O.B.* 1926, (repr. 1974: Memoirer og Breve XLVII).

"Brøndsted, P.O.", in *Salmonsens Konversationsleksikon*, vol. IV, Copenhagen 1916, 182-83. (The article is written by H.A. Kjær).

"Brøndsted, P.O.", in S. Cedergreen Bech (ed.), *Dansk Biografisk Leksikon*, III, 1979, 33-36 (The biography is written by Gorm Rode and K. Friis Johansen).

"P.O. Brøndsted", in Poul Johs. Jensen and Leif Grane (ed.), *Københavns Universitet 1479-1979*, Bind VIII, København 1992, 294-300 (The article is written by Ivan Boserup).

Byron's Letters and Journals. Edited by Leslie A. Marchand, 1973 (1994).

Cockerell, Ch.R., *Travels in Southern Europe and the Levant 1810-1817, the Journal of C.R. Cockerell*, Ed. by S.P. Cockerell, Edinburgh, 1904.

Davenport, W., *Historical portraiture of leading events in the life of Ali Pacha, Vizier of Epirus surnamed the Lion, in a Series of Designs drawn by W. Davenport and engraved by G. Hunt with a biographical sketch.* London, 1823.

Dodwell, Ed., *A Classical and Topographical Tour through Greece during the Years 1801, 1895 and 1806*, 1-2, London 1819.

Dupré, L. *Voyages à Athènes et à Constantinople ou Collection de Portraits, de Vues et de costumes Grecs et Ottomans.* Par L. Dupré, élève de David. Paris, 1825.

Haugsted, Ida, *Dream and Reality, Danish antiquaries, architects and artists in Greece*, London, 1996. (Chapters 1-3 offer a detailed and excellent presentation of Brøndsted and his achievements).

Hobhouse, John Cam, A Journey through Albania and the other Provinces of Turkey and Europe, London 1813.

Holland, H., *Travels in the Ionian Isles, Albania, Thessaly, Macedonia etc. during the years 1812 and 1813*, London 1815.

Hughes, T.S., *Travels in Sicily, Greece, and Albania*, I-II. London, 1820.

—, *Travels in Greece and Albania*, I-II. 2nd ed. with considerable addition, London 1830. (Cf. the Preface: "Moreover, by enlarging the second volume, he [the author] has been enabled to lay before the reader a complete narrative of the Life of and the Death of that extraordinary personage Ali Pasha of Ioannina, together with a concise account of the Revolution in which he bore a distinguished part, and which has given independence to Greece.")
[Hughes and C.R. Cockerell visited Ali Pasha in January 1814. Cockerell's drawings from this visit are used as illustrations in Hughes' text.]

Manzour, Ibrajim efendi, *Mémoirs sur la Grèce et l'Albanie pendant le gouvernement d'Ali pasha*, Paris 1828.

(Malte-Brun), Ali Hissas di Tepeleni. Bassà di Jannina. Prospetto storico e politico del Sig. Malte-Brun. [We have not been able to see this sketch in the original French.] In the Florence Antologia. *The North American Review* No XLII; New Series No XVII for January 1824. Boston, 1824.

Pouqueville, F.C.H.L., *Voyage en Morée, à Constantinople, en Albanie et dans plusieurs autres parties de l'Empire Ottomanes*, London 1805.

—, *Voyage dans la Grèce avec cartes, vues et figures*, 1-6, Paris 1826-27

Stackelberg, O.M. von, *Der Apollotempel zu Bassae in Arcadien und die daselbst ausgegrabenen Bildwerke*, Rom 1926.

—, *Costumes et Usages des Peuples de la Grèce Moderne gravés d'apres les dessin exécutés sur les lieux en 1811* par le Baron O.M. de Stackelberg et publiés à Rome 1825.

—, *Trachten und Gebraüche der Neugriechen* von O.M. Baron v. Stackelberg, Berlin, 1831.

—, *La Grèce.* Vues pittoresques et topographiques dessinées par O.M. Baron de Stackelberg, Paris 1834.

—, *Schilderung seines Lebens und seiner Reisen in Italien und Griechenland.* Nach Tagebücher und Briefen dargestellt von N. von Stackelberg. Heidelberg, 1883.

In marble-paved pavilion, where a spring
Of living water from the centre rose,
Whose bubbling did a genial freshness fling,
and soft voluptuous couches breathed repose,
Ali reclined, — a man of war and woes;
Yet in his lineaments ye cannot trace,
While gentleness her milder radiance throws
Along that aged venerable face,
The deeds that lurk beneath, and stain him with disgrace.

(Byron's *Childe Harold* (1812), Canto II, Stanza 62.
Byron and John Hobhouse visited Ali Pasha in 1809).

5. Portrait of Ali Pasha. Drawn by C.R. Cockerell. The Gennadius Library, Athens.

On the Author's interviews with Ali Pacha of Joanina, in the autumn of 1812; with some particulars of Epirus, and the Albanians of the present day.

Ali of Tepeleni, a man who by his extraordinary qualities, as well as by his crimes, exercised during more than half a century, an unbounded influence over the finest provinces of Greece, and upon the recent events which have changed the face of those countries, once so beautiful, and even still so interesting — was, inquestionably, one of the most remarkable personages in the vast Ottoman Empire, the downfall of which prepared for a century past, has only been delayed to our days by the reciprocal jealousy, and the want of energy and moral dignity in the rulers of Europe. This man, whom history will, doubtless, distinguish as a kind of physiological phenomenon, descended from a Musselman family of Albania, if not of obscure at least of middling rank. Notwithstanding innumerable obstacles, he established himself as the absolute despot over the finest European provinces of the Turkish Empire, and a population of two millions of inhabitants. Daring, and fertile in resources, he knew how to support his usurpations, and his crimes, by an army of about thirty five thousand men — excellent troops, at least for carrying on war in those regions, and against the Turks, — and by all those means which immense treasures supply in every country, but more particularly in Turkey.

Ali Pacha, the most consummate Albanian of his time, alone knew how to solve a problem extremely difficult — that of uniting under his banners a people the most savage and the most marauding in Europe, divided before his days into a thousand distinct and independent tribes, who plundered and murdered each other without ceasing. He alone was the first who knew how to overawe them all, to terminate their particular feuds, and to subjugate them all beneath his sceptre of iron, so that it would be strictly true to say — that Ali Pacha, for the last twenty years of his long career, was the sole robber in his states, and that there was more personal security in travelling there than in most of the southern countries of Europe. After all, it appears to me, that a single privileged plunderer is better than a multitude of subaltern tyrants, not only for travellers, but also for the inhabitants of any country whatever; at least some arrangement can be made with one only, but there is no stipulating with a host of petty plunderers; besides despotism, though in its nature monstrous and sterile, still occasionally produces something good, whilst anarchy, the pest of all social order, never brings forth any thing profitable whatsoever. This truth, I fear, must serve as a consolation, not only beyond the Adriatic, but even elsewhere. Thus it was that Ali Pacha, his exploits and his family were, during my stay in Greece, one of the principal themes of the popular songs, which we often heard and in almost all the provinces of Greece and Epirus; from Taygetus to Olympus and the Acroceraunian mountains as far as Carystos in Euboea.

If I had seen Ali Pacha on my first arrival in Greece, I should not have known, perhaps, either to have comprehended him well, or to have drawn any advantage from it for my own meditations. But I saw him on my return from a stay of three years in that interesting country, when I had but too well learnt to understand the great influence of that extraordinary person, throughout the whole of Greece. Speaking then, with some facility, the modern Greek, I had occasion to converse with him during several days without the aid of an interpreter and even under circumstances sufficiently *piquantes* and, I own, I was then struck with the originality of the man. I will attempt here to give some parts of these conversations, preceding them by a few brief observations on the Albanians of the present day, and on the life of Ali Pacha, up to the period I saw him at Prevesa, towards the end of the year 1812.

Among the tribes who now inhabit Epirus and Greece the Albanians, οἱ Ἀλβανίται, or as it is pronounced in Greece οἱ Ἀρϐανίται, are those who at once command the stranger's notice; at first by their picturesque dress resembling the war costume of the Roman soldiers, in the time of the Emperors, next, and yet more strikingly, by their temperament and their demeanour, which differ as much from those of the Greeks as from those of the Turks. In general their bodies are slender but very nervous; the complexion pale; the profile and features well expressed; the head mostly of the oval shape; the forehead high, but

narrow and projecting; the eyes small, but very lively, and even ardent, which often withdraw into their deep orbits. Their look has almost always something decided and even ferocious in it, and I never saw a single Albanian, with that languishing and soft air, which is so common amongst the Turks. The mouth is small, with very fine teeth; the chin large and projecting; the hands and feet small, but very nervous; and even the most slender amongst them have the legs well rounded and proportioned (*Sura teres*) These complexional qualities are still more conspicuous by their variegated and striking national costume, which it would be superfluous to describe, now that we have several correct

6-7 (facing page), 8 (right):
Ali Pasha's hunting-barge, drawn
by L. Dupré, Butrinto, 1819.
Details showing Ali's Albanian
guardsmen. The Gennadius Library,
Athens.

colour engravings of it by different English travellers (a)[1] I shall merely observe that this costume produces a peculiar effect on the *bust* of the
Albanian especially in three respects: that the neck is always open, that
the hair of the occiput waves freely over the shoulders, and that the sinciput, which they always shave (b)[2] is covered with a small calotte of
cloth or of red velvet, ornamented with a silk tuft of another colour. The
women, — who never shave the forepart of the head, but dispose their,
generally, fine hair in a number of tresses, which fall upon the shoulders and the back, — wear, also, the calotte, but larger than that of the
men; they cover it with as many pieces of gold and silver coin as they

9. Woman from the neighbourhood of Thebes. She wears a calotte and a shoulder cape, covered with coins. Drawing by Otto Magnus von Stackelberg, 1811. The Gennadius Library, Athens.

can procure, amongst which are often found ancient medals; and every traveller curious in such relicts will frequently have occasion to treat with the young Albanian damsels for some pieces of their calottes, which they, in general, give up cheerfully, in receiving in exchange (that being understood) modern pieces of much larger size, provided they do not regard the coins requested as a species of talisman, which is sometimes the case amongst the common people. This has happened to me, especially in Boeotia in the villages adjacent to Livadia and the Lake Copais where I have often seen very fine ancient medals, of the kind represented in the 8 vignettes of this work [now lost, see Pl. 9] without being able to obtain a single one, owing to the superstitious idea I have just stated. Such a calotte, covered with gold and silver pieces, carefully arranged upon a handsome head, produces by no means a bad effect. I have had several in my hands which were worth about two hundred piastres; accordingly a young Albanian girl considers it as an essential part of her dower; for after marriage she ceases to wear this heavy ornament of the head, and sacrifices it, of course, to her husband; and it may happen, sometimes, that the Albanian youth, who regards with tenderness the head of his fair one, may not be altogether indifferent to the rich calotte which covers it.

It is indubitably an effect of the extraordinary talents of Ali Pacha, that this race of men, singularly active, bold and warlike, have, in the last half century, been converted from a people of robbers and semi-savages into a nation of warriors, who play in the present day a remarkable, and even brilliant, part amongst the tribes inhabiting the vast Ottoman Empire. For the renown of the Albanians for bravery causes them to be sought after by the Turkish governments, even from the remotest provinces, for the purpose of enrolling them amongst their troops, or in their guards, and as the Swiss were formerly, and still are in many countries of the west; so, in the present day, the Albanians are established in the Levant, not only in several provinces of European Turkey, but, also, in Asia-Minor, in Syria, in Egypt, and elsewhere.

These successes have rendered up, so to express it, the Albanians of our time to the historic page; and several English travellers have lately devoted themselves to researches on the origin of this people (c)[3]. These researches, besides being very difficult from the deficiency of all national literature of those tribes, do not enter in the plan of this work. I merely observe that, from a careful comparison of the migrations of the middling ages into those countries, with the present idiom of the Albanians, it would, according to my idea, result that the actual inhabitants of Epirus are descended from a mixture of the natives (before and during the establishment of the ancient Greeks in Epirus) with the Illyrian tribes, who came from the north, as by degrees the provincial Roman government, emanating from Constantinople, fell into decadency. I should even believe that the beginning of the emigration of the

Illyrians into Epirus, dates from an epoch much earlier, that is from the dreadful destruction of Epirus by the Roman army, after the conquest of Macedonia by Paulus Emilius (d).[4]

It is, especially, from the study of the dialects of the *Skipetarik* (as the Albanians themselves term their idiom) that elucidations might be looked for on the subject, and it would be very inportant for the history of this people, that the interesting researches, commenced by colonel Martin Leake (e),[5] were continued. In other respects there is not much inducement to study an idiom, which offers absolutely nothing resembling an appearance of literature; since the Skipetarik or language of the Albanians is completely oral, and they are obliged to make use of Greek characters in writing it.

Every christian Albanian who has enjoyed any education understands the modern Greek, often better than his native langue. All literary instruction, in the religious and other schools, is conveyed in modern Greek, except with some tribes, who for many centuries have embraced Islamism, to which, by the by, they do not adhere very strictly. Notwithstanding the total change in the political relations which anciently subsisted between the two people; in general, the moral affinity of the Albanians with the Greeks of our days yet bears much resemblance to those of the Epiriotes with the ancient Greeks. For the Greeks are still their instructors in every thing that regards civilization, or relates to the resources, feeble and poor, without doubt, of a cultivated state in this country. The absolute defect of attempts to elevate the language in question to the rank of a written language, or at least, to make of it a depository of opinions and of individual ideas, — a defect so sensibly felt amongst a race of men, consisting of more than a million of individuals, in constant intercourse, political or otherwise with two great nations (the Greeks and the Turks), each of which possesses a literature of its own — this moral phenomenon evidently announces a peculiarly remarkable absence of perception and of ideas, a great sterility of mind; it also appears to me that a disposition of the intellectual faculties to civilization, a certain aptitude of the soul or rather, according to the phraseology of a modern system, the organ of perfectibility, forms the inestimable prerogative of the Greek as opposed to the Albanian; and if, after the manner of the ancients, I may here avail myself of a comparison I would say — that the latter resembles the former as the wolf resembles the dog of a certain species. The

10. Albanian soldier. Drawing by Otto Magnus von Stackelberg, 1811. The Gennadius Library, Athens.

Albanian is prudent, dexterous, and active in all the ordinary relations of life, in all the combinations and affairs which do not exceed his intelligence; he is faithful, sure and persevering in the service of him who has known how to recognize his attachment, and that in a manner which surpasses belief; but he is deep, cunning, dissimulant and cruel as a tiger towards his enemies.

These traits seems to me the most national and the most universal in respect to the character and physiognomy of this people in general.

What can be done with them, particularly in war, has in our days been put in dreadful evidence by Ali Pacha, the most perfect model of the Albanian that ever existed, and, if I may so express it, the flower of Albanism.

We have lately seen that head fall[6] bleached with years of crime and charged with the execrations of thousands of his victims amongst the Greek population of his states; — but it was not the crimes af Ali Pacha that conducted him to his fate, — that, indeed, would have been consoling to humanity, — unhappily quite the reverse, for it was the well combined, and constantly followed, system of his offences which had elevated him, by degrees, to the power of a formidable oriental despot; one sole vice ruined him — his *avarice*; for that was the true cause of the catastrophe of Ali Pacha. It rendered him blind to such a degree, that, when shut up in the Castle of Joanina with a handful of his faithful followers, he still nourished the mad hope of extricating himself, without opening his treasures to the Greeks and the Albanians, who were equally capable of saving or selling him for gold.

The circumstances that led to the fate of the modern tyrant of Epirus, absolutely remind me of those which preceded the fall of the last unworthy tyrant of ancient Macedonia — Perseus, whose sordid avarice caused, accordingly to Plutarch (f)[7] the good fortune of Paulus Emilius and his Romans; just as the blind obstinacy of Ali Vizier lately affected that of Courshid Pacha and his Turks, who were too feeble to chain the old royal tiger of the Albanians, if this vice, his domestic demon, his veritable *Kakodaemon* had not come to their aid.

After the two interesting narratives given us by Mr. D. Holland and Mr. Pougueville (g)[8] I should not be able to relate any thing new on the life of Ali Pacha. I shall merely proceed to enumerate some facts of it, amongst the most remarkable and the most adopted to display the character of that surprising man, since *to represent him himself such as I saw him*, is my principal design here.

Ali Pacha was born in 1740 at Tepeleni, a small town and district about fourteen or fifteen leagues to the north of Joanina; his father Vely was governor, or Pacha, but of an inferior rank, the third class, and in that station ruled over Tepeleni and the small territories dependent on it. His resources were slender; he had no treasures, his influence at Constantinople was null and his power, in consequence very feeble. He died when his son Ali Bey was but fifteen or sixteen years of age. Albania was then divided into a considerable number of small *Pachalics*, the petty tyrants of which were constantly disputing with and slaughtering each other. They regarded the domains of young Ali, yet a minor, as an easy prey, and persecuted him accordingly. His mother, an enterprising and courageous woman, being no longer in a situation to support the rights of her son, was constrained to fly with him from Tepeleni. The Gardikians (inhabitants of a town and mountainous district some leagues from Tepeleni) — who were the special and sworn foes of Ali's family, endeavoured to entrap both mother and son, who were surprised in a village by a party of those people in ambush. Ali escaped, but his mother was taken, and treated in the most unworthy manner. They, however, afterwards, released her on receiving a ransom, and from that time, as the power of Ali progressively developed itself, she ceased not to remind him of his promise to avenge her on the Gardikians. — Forty years after he took that vengeance in a manner truly horrible and every way worthy of his character!

Supported by some Turkish Governors of the neighbouring districts, the youthful Ali was again rendered master of Tepeleni, and his possessions. At twenty years of age, and considered the finest young man in all Albania (many popular songs celebrate him as such) he entered into the service of Coul-Pacha, governor of Berat, who, it appeared, took umbrage of his ambition and warlike spirit; Ali, in consequence, retired suddenly from Berat with a few faithful followers. The negotiations which he entered upon, during his absence, with the governor of Berat, were so succesful that the latter gave him his daughter in marriage.

His two eldest sons, Muctar and Vely (exiled in 1821 to Asia Minor and there decapitated by the grand Seignior's orders) were the fruits of this marriage. During my stay in Greece Muctar had the rank of of a pacha, and was commander in chief of his father's troops; he usually resided at Joanina. Vely in 1812 was still Pacha of the Morea, but his continual extorsions, and the incessant complaints carried to Constantinople against him, by the Greeks of the Morea (backed by the *sterling* argument in their purses) prevailed upon the Grand Seignor to recall and degrade him to the much less important government of some inferior districts in Thessaly, where he had his residence at Larisa, from whence he was sent, in 1821, to Asia Minor.

The power of Ali was yet but very limited, when a bold enterprise against the Pacha of Joanina, a weak and timid man, rendered him master of that city, and of considerable resources. He knew how to palliate this usurpation at Constantinople, and to obtain of the Porte a firman in quality of Pacha of Joanina. In the mean time the good fortune and personal endowments of Ali, began to draw upon him the notice of the Albanian tribes, even the most remote; many of whom — who, notwithstanding a species of capitulation with the Porte, found themselves constantly exposed to the vexations of the neighbouring governors, voluntarily united themselves with Ali, and sought protection and fortune beneath his banner.

Occupied for some successive years in consolidating his powers in Albania, Ali contrived to procure from Constantinople, first the lease of the greatest part of the Custom-Houses (Giumbroicke) of the neighbouring provinces, and afterwards the title of *Dervini-Pacha* in Roumelie. These posts, especially that of Derveni Pacha, were of great importance to him, not less for securing his possessions in Albania than for increasing his influence in the provinces properly Greek. Since the Dervini are the military passages and stations in the mountains by which communication of the provinces, or of one district, with another, is maintained. It is easy to comprehend that the occupation of all these passages by the troops of Ali Pacha must have furnished him with frequent occasions and pretexts to intermeddle in the affairs of other Pachas, and governors, for the purpose of gaining over the people and to know all that was going forward.

It was thus, to cite but one example, that, in this character of Dervini Pacha, he insinuated himself into the rich and fine province of Thessaly, where he was already all powerful ere his son Vely was established at Larissa in 1812.

I cannot help thinking, besides, that it was one of Ali Pacha's greatest errors, not to have vigorously supported his son in the station of principal Pacha of the Morea. Vely was a fine man, of considerable capability, he had even talent — and of a very agreeable conversation, but exceedingly profligate; his excesses led him into great expenses. To meet these he was, doubtless, obliged to drain the purses of the richest Greeks of the Morea and their consequent remonstrances to the Porte caused his banishment to a petty government in Thessaly, as previously related.

11. Ismaël Bey and Mehemet Pasha, son of Vely, grandsons of Ali from Tepelen. Drawing by L. Dupré. The Gennadius Library, Athens.

A Turk of distinguished family in Anatolia, Mehemed of Adramyth, was then appointed Pacha over the Morea. I saw him twice on some business at Tripolizza, in the month of October 1812. He was evidently an enemy to the House of Ali Pacha, and began the exercise of his new functions by cutting off the heads of two Greeks, minions of Vely, and who after the latter's departure for Larissa still passed for his agents in Peloponnesus. Ali of Joanina certainly was able to have maintained his son in the Morea, if his avarice had not withheld him from opening his purse, as it is essential to do at Constantinople; for it is thus affairs of state go on at that Sublime Porte, worm-eaten enough, without doubt, but still propped up, well or ill, by two caryatids of expanded shoulders — the *jealousy* and *bad faith* of christians. To return to Ali Pacha.

In 1798 Ali marched at the head of 15,000 Albanians against Viddin, and the rebel Pasvan Oglou who was there fortified; he commanded the second corps of the army in an attack upon that place. On this occasion he was named Vizier, or Pacha of the first rank (of three tails).

His father in law Coul Pacha of Berat was dead, and the successor they had given him in that government, Ibrahim Pacha soon disagreed with Ali; the latter however judged it more prudent to make it up with him, for that time. To this end he entered into negotiations the result of which was — the double marriage of the two sons of Ali, Muctar and Vely, with the two daughters of Ibrahim.

The French expedition to Egypt, under the general in chief Bonaparte, and the consequent hostilities of the Porte against France, led Ali to take possession of Prevesa, the most important point upon the terra firma which was yet, as an ancient Venetian dependancy, occupied by the French. Towards the end of the year 1798, with a numerous force infinitely superior, he gained a victory over the French near the ruins of the ancient city of Nicopolis; he took the town of Prevesa, and sent to Constantinople as many heads as he could have cut off, from the French and the Greeks, who had fought against him (gg).[9] The manner too in which he treated the town of Prevesa seemed quite inconsistent and unreasonable.

He openly ill used the Greek inhabitants of the place, that is to say the most industrious and most useful part of its population, who from 10 or 12,000 souls, of which it was composed before its conquest by Ali, have since been reduced to a third of that number. Some well informed Greeks at Joanina assured me, that the Vizier had been determined by political, and also by personal, views to harass the people of Prevesa, in order to expel them from thence by degrees; they pretended to know, that he looked upon the place as the most convenient point for embarking himself, his family and his treasures, in the event of his being menaced by any unexpected storm from Constantinople, and that he desired, in consequence, to occupy Prevesa exclusively with his Albanians; the only people he could rely upon in such an extremity. Events have turned out differently, but the importance which he obviously attached to the capture of Prevesa, and the extreme care he took to have it fortified at all points, and to settle himself there commodiously, as he built two palaces for that purpose, these appear to justify the opinion of the Greeks on the subject, when I was at Prevesa, and at Joanina, in the winter of 1812-1813.

After the conquest of Prevesa Ali passed into Acarnania, took Vanitsa and Carlili, and expelled the petty governors established in different places, subjugated the whole province, and moreover obtained from Constantinople the firman which confirmed him in this new usurpation.

The whole of southern Albania already formed the nucleus of his states; for the brave and highspirited inhabitants of the mountains of Suly — those hero-robbers, who (scarcely forming a tribe of 5 or 6000 souls, all Albanian christians) resisted for sixteen years the power of Ali — had since 1803 been driven from their native hearths. The wars of Ali Pacha against Suly, the heroic defence of its inhabitants, and the final submission of these mountains, form a picture so diversified and interesting, that they merit to be compared to those of the ancient Messenians against the Spartans; they especially present the greatest analogy with the defense and the taking of Ira in Messenia such as Pausanias has described it to us.(h)[10]

As soon as Ali, at the commencement of the present century, believed himself sufficiently powerful, he sought a quarrel with the father in law of his two sons, Ibrahim Pacha of Berat, who, in concert with his ally Muhammed Pacha of Delvino, resisted for some time the puissance of Ali, but the usual good fortune of the latter did not forsake him in this infamous war of usurpation neither. He finally routed the united troops of the two unfortunate Pachas, who both fell into his hands, and were imprisoned by his orders in the fortress of Joanina. These events which augmented the states af Ali Pacha by a population of 300,000 souls, had taken place some time previous to my arrival at Joanina, towards the end of the year 1812.

The fall of Delvino led to that of Argyrocastro and Gardiki, of that same Gardiki whose inhabitants, renowned in Albania as enterprising and warlike, had forty years before persecuted the young Ali and his mother, and so indignantly treated the latter. He ordered the entire population of Gardiki, about six thousand souls, to be dispersed to work as slaves on the different roads, and other constructions, in southern Albania. Their Beys, or chiefs of the most distinguished families[11] were sent to the prisons of Joanina.

From the six thousand Gardikians, eight hundred were selected from the families which had been established in Gardiki forty years or more, when that people had dishonoured his mother. These eight hundred persons were assembled in the same place, in a Khani (caravansary) near Argyrocastro. The pacha himself repaired thither in his carriage,[12] attended by a troop of soldiers. From a list, which he held in his hand, he ordered fifty individuals, whom he considered as the least culpable to come out of the Khani, and commanded them to rejoin those miserable thousands of their countrymen, already dispersed to the slavish labours I have spoken of. The Khani was then closed, the troops posted upon the walls, and roofs, of the building, and the Pacha himself gave signal of carnage by firing a pistol ...

Nearly all the seven hundred and fifty Gardikians were murdered by the musquetery! some of those unfortunates, who had contrived to hide themselves in the building, were afterwards massacred at the edge of the sabre. The bodies of those sad victims of a monster's vengeance, were left in the Khani, which was from that time deserted. In the autumn of 1812 their unburied bones still remained there.

Ali caused a stone to be placed above the entrance of the edifice, bearing the following inscription in modern Greek:

> Thus Perish All
> Who Dare
> Oppose Themselves
> To
> Ali of Tepelini
> Or
> Dishonour His Family

Some years after the French expedition to Egypt, when Bonaparte, then first consul had been again victorious in Italy, it appears that proposals were made on the part of the French government to Ali Pacha, with a view of inducing him to make a diversion against the Turks in favour of France. Some Greeks of my acquaintance of Joanina, thought that the bait offered to Ali has been the crown of Greece, or rather of Romelia. It even appears that he did not, at all, look with indifference upon the price offered for a cooperation of the kind. But fearing to become himself a victim of it, — and the confederacy of the Porte with England justified him — he, all at once, changed his policy and again placed himself in open hostilities with the French, and even (as they assured me at Joanina) confided to the Turks and the Albanian chiefs the tempting proposals which had been made to him, asking them at the same time, with his accustomed burst of laughter, "what they thought of that fool of a French consul (ὁ τρέλλος κόνσουλος φράνκος) wishing to make Ali-Vizir his *Vice-Consul* at Prevesa?" In effect Ali evinced by his subsequent conduct towards the French established at St. Maure [Leukas], at Corfu, and in the other Ionian Isles, by his proceedings, sometimes harsh and haughty, at other times kind in appearance but always deceitful at the bottom, that he had no desire to make himself what he termed *a French Vice-Consul at Prevesa.*

By his bad faith, and his profound hypocrisy he had particularly irritated the Emperor Napoleon who speaking with the Greek patricians af the Ionian Isles[13] — sent to Paris in 1806 to compliment him as Emperor — of the Islanders connections with their treacherous neighbour, amongst other things, told them, "that it was, assuredly, one of his political views *some day to deliver his visiting card at the residence of Monsieur le Brigand de Tepeleni"*[14] — There can be little doubt but Napoleon really meant, one day or other, to have transmitted this visiting card, backed by a *complement* of sixty thousand men, if providence had not otherwise disposed of his destiny.

Nothing struck me so much in Albania, as that species of admiration, and personal attachment, with which their tyrant had inspired the Albanians. Their sentiment manifested itself in an unequivocal manner, not merely amongst his civil officers, amongst his *Tzucadares*, or guards (very fine and choice troops) and others who had easy access to his person, but also with the great mass of the army and the people. This phenomenon would have been inconceivable to me, if I had not so closely seen Ali himself.

Every man who possesses virtuous sentiments and moral qualities, easily imagines that these same qualities — the only that are positively and unreservedly good in the human character — ought, also, to form the only titles to the obedience and esteem of his fellow men. — But it is not thus. Man is a being so various and void of reason that taken in the mass and considered in the fine (I mean in this insulated part of our existence), he appears to me rather a complicated and intelligent machine, than a moral being. Endowed, as I am, with the most unbounded reliance in the Divine Providence, I firmly believe that Man is a moral creature *by his destiny*. I even see that august destination imprinted in the most signal manner on some individuals of our species, happily organized and born under fortunate auspices; but for what regards man in general I see nothing which explains to me the enigma of existence in that respect; neither in the history of times past nor in the page of daily experience. I behold, rather, the great mass of mankind almost always victims to individual power, which, by its agency, imposes upon the multitude to that degree, that they submit, without reserve, to become the blind instruments of tyranny. If the history of the most enlightened people of the ancient world presents us this sad spectacle; if it is the same with most of the nations who in our days call themselves civilized; farther — if it is true that despotism stifles in its victims even the consciousness of object state into which it has plunged them — surely, we ought not to be astonished that a people scarcely emerged from a savage state, scarcely enlightened by the first glimmering of civilization, should have followed, during half a century, the sanguinary banners of a frightful tyrant, who, notwithstanding his crimes, which he did not even take pains to conceal, possessed so many qualities fitted to impose upon his slaves, and to inspire them with admiration for his person.

It is worth while to pause a moment, to contemplate, what may be termed the machine which moved an extraordinary man, who had so decided an ascendancy over the whole of Greece. The remarks which follow were communicated to me by Greeks of Arta, and of Joanina, who had lived much with Ali Pacha, and who had the opportunity of closely observing him during the twenty years which, at least, formed the most active part of his political career.

Ali had, preeminently, the talent of placing himself on his guard against his immediate ministers and other officers, and of preserving himself with invariable address, independent of their influence.

No person ever enjoyed the slightest ascendancy over him, nor did he ever allow himself to be drawn into the counsels of any of his dependants whoever it was; still less was he disposed to admit them as decisive measures; at the same time he knew how to attach every detail of any importance, exclusively to his own person.

His untiring activity, and astonishing memory were the chief resources that enabled him to sustain this difficult part. The account of any affair what ever, frequently even of minor importance, having been received by the Vizier with apparent satisfaction — lo!, all at once, often some months after, and when one would have thought the affair in question almost forgotten, all the parties concerned were sent for, and assembled together at the palace. These individuals, sometimes simple peasants, or other of the common people, admitted to the Pacha's audience, and at first awed by his presence, or dazzled by the magnificence of the apartments of a grand Turkish Seignior, were soon put perfectly at their ease by the smooth and gracious words of the Pacha, by the manner full of affability and kindness, in which he knew how to talk with them of their native mountain, or village, frequently too of their own families and nearest kindred. For Ali's memory was singularly faithful, even for things of that sort; and the turbulent state of his youth had placed him in the situation of acquiring a knowledge of Albania to its most unfrequented places. A Greek from Arta said to me one day, in speaking of the Pacha's peculiar talent for questioning people: "I know not how it is, but, in general, the Vizier so contrives it, *that it is impossible to tell a falsehood in his presence.*" Having thus learnt of those simple individuals, all he desired to know on the subject, he compared their testimony with the details in the report of his officers and wo! to whoever had sought to deceive him. By this habit, constantly followed, of calling before him all the persons interested in an affair, he seldom missed his aim.

Another advantage accrued from it, which, although secondary, was yet of importance to him. These poor people, having been well treated, and often well recompensed, on returning to their homes, published everywhere his praises; they extolled on all sides his justice, his penetration, his goodness, his affability, his benevolent behaviour etc.

It may be conceived that in Albania, particularly, such conduct on the part of Ali, was perfectly well calculated; since the attachment of a half-savage people to their master is, by no means, the result of reflection on subjects relating to the nature and goodness of his government. This reflection does not exist even in the most civilized nations, except with a very small number of individuals. The attachment of an uncultivated people for their chief is always, and in the first tie, the effect of *tradition* and of *custom* next of the subject's opinion (most generally, too, false or exaggerated) of the *personal qualities of his ruler.* — Now, Ali having known from the commencement of his long career, how to insinuate himself into the good graces of the Albanians, and sustaining his part as the most consumate political actor in all Turkey, my astonishment ceases at having beheld, with my own eyes, this horrible despot, not withstanding his monstrous and measureless crimes, enjoying a popularity to such an extent, that it would not be possible to wish a greater share to the most virtuous prince in existence. It seemed to me, that these sentiments of the common people towards the Vizier, were blended with a superstitious feeling, whimsical enough. They went as far as to excuse the crimes of the despot, consoling themselves, for those openly committed, by saying that *such was the will of God*; that the deeds of the Pacha were directed *by the hand of Providence* etc. I have witnessed several instances of this strange and devious disposition of the lower classes; and I will quote one here which peculiarly struck me.

On leaving Prevesa for the interior of Albania, I had with me an Albanian of the Vizier's guard, who had been ordered by the latter to attend me, wherever I chose to go, and to be careful to my interest. This soldier was called Dimo of Argyrocastro, a fine courageous young man, and equally intelligent as faithful. I afterwards dismissed him at Sajades, perfectly satisfied with his services. As he was a christian and spoke the Greek very well, I often conversed with him of the Pacha's actions, and of the events in Albania, which he was well aquainted with. His two first compaigns had been made against the troops of Ali, but having been taken prisoner at the capture of Argyrocastro, his native place, he obtained the Pacha's pardon and entered into his service. This gallant young man often recounted to me, without the smallest reserve, all the horrors which had been perpetrated at the capture of Argyrocastro, by the soldiers of the conqueror. The whole of his family, his mother, his two sisters, and his eldest brother, had been massacred in the sacking of the town: his uncle was beheaded eight days after, by order of the Vizier. Above all, he spoke with an emotion, truly touching, of the deplorable fate of his mother and his two sisters — whom he tenderly loved. Who would not have imagined that horrors like these which had filled the soul of this honest man with bitterness and sorrow, would at the same time have filled it with an unconquerable hate against the tyrant — the principal cause of so many losses? I was much astonished to observe quite the contrary. The disasters of his country, and of his family, had so struck and bewildered his imagination, that he rather accused the obstinacy and mad perseverance of his countrymen, than the Pacha's cruelty, as the cause of them. In short, the fall of Argyrocastro had fully persuaded him that the Vizier was invincible, and had a just title to the domination over the whole of

Teraglio di Ali Bascha apresso di Nicopolis.

7. Nicopoli

Seraglio dell ali Bassa.

1810. 28 Aug.

12. Prevesa. The Serail of Ali Pasha. Drawn by Carl Haller von Hallerstein, October, 28th, 1811. Bibliothèque Nationale et Universitaire de Strasbourg.

Albania. A little time after, he kissed the blood-stained hand of the destroyer of his country and became *his man*. He spoke of all this with tears in his eyes, but with the most sincere resignation, evidently confounding the will of heaven with that of the Pacha! It may easily be conceived that, in my then situation it was not for me to combat this gross confusion in the head of a worthy and honest young man, who served me so well.

It has often been held that despotism depraves the human heart, which is very true, but it is equally true that it perplexes and confounds the understanding. The first effect is perceived in contemplating the Despot himself and his privileged slaves. The second effect is chiefly manifested in the slaves not privileged and in the mass of the people; the one is the abasement moral, the other the abasement intellectual; each and both proceeding from despotism, are equally deplorable; they are companions, like the chill and the heat of a fever, they deprave existence, and brutalize humanity.

Ali, by his personal qualifications, had equally imposed upon his subjects of a superior rank, upon his immediate officers Turks and Greeks etc; but their sentiments for him must, necessarily, have been so much the less sincere, as it was more in their power to perceive some of the wheels of his political machine; to be acquainted with his views, his tyrannical impetuosity, his dreadful choler, which often broke out in spite of his profound dissimulation and notwithstanding the amenity which he usually studied to shed upon his conversation. The sentiment of the Albanian people for their master was a sincere attachment produced by habit and astonishment; that of the higher orders of his followers, Turks and Greeks, for the despot a calculation of fear. All classes and individuals concurred in a blind obedience, and I found the comparison just which an intelligent young Greek made to me one day, as we were talking tête-à-tête, of the situation of his country — "Ali Pacha", said he, is like a monstrous spider, which has spread over the whole of Albania, and a part of Greece a magic web, so fine and complicated that it only requires a slight movement in any thread of the web, to draw to the centre and seat of the monster the thousands of individuals who move on its surface, with a freedom which consists only in appearance".

I did not see Ali in his capital, but at Prevesa where he was, with a numerous troop, when I arrived there, for the second time, on my return from Greece in November 1812. My first visit to him was, in a certain manner, one of necessity. I had gone with my companion the young count de Lunzi,[15] the day after our arrival to reexamine the ruins of the ancient city of Nicopolis. During our absence, the Vizier, having learnt that two strangers, Franks, had arrived the day before, sent one of his guards, to inquire of the poor Greek family by whom we had been hospitally received, who those strangers were; a commission which was executed in rather a ferocious manner; as if the Pacha was displeased, at their having already lodged twenty four hours, two Franks who were unknown to him. Thus, on our return from Nicopolis, we found the poor family in a state of uneasiness on our account. I, therefore, at once, determined to endeavour to procure an audience of the Vizier next day if possible. I declined the offer made by a Greek merchant, for whom I had brought some letters of recommendation, to introduce me, on account of his extreme timidity; as I foresaw an humiliating scene, should this poor man find himself before the Vizier; for I had already had frequent occasions to remark, that the Turkish seigniors always grew more inflated, in proportion as the persons in their presence become more submissive and servile.

Every independent and honest mind feels itself ill at ease with a pussillanimous and abased companion, as we seem in some measure to participate in his humiliation. I, therefore, preferred to be presented by the English resident Mr. F.—[16] having had the pleasure of knowing him previously at Zante, his native place. Mr F.— proposed to introduce me, as an English traveller, but this I declined for two reasons — first because I never like to pass for what I am not, next because I promised myself some amusing conversation, or some strange question on the Vizier's part, to whom my country must have been as unknowm as the people in the moon to Nicolas Klim in the voyage of our *Holberg*.[17] We merely agreed not to mention a word of the war, which still continued in 1812 between England and Denmark, by way of escaping all remarks from the Pacha upon an accredited Englishman's introducing a Dane to his presence.

The following day on arriving at the hour fixed by the Pacha, we found the palace full of soldiers, to the amount of about 4,000 men, whom he had brought with him from Joanina; they formed extremely varied and animated groupes in the court of the palace, and were most of them employed in cleaning their arms. We were told that the Vizier was to pass them in review in the afternoon.

On entering the edifice, we crossed at first some of those spacious, gloomy and vacant rooms that usually precede the apartments of a Turkish grandée, but which bear more resemblance to the compartments of a granary, or, rather, of a barrack than to the antichamber of a great personage. We only meet with some twenty of the Vizier's

13. Janissary from Ioannina, drawn by Otto Magnus von Stackelberg, 1811. The Gennadius Library, Athens.

Tzucadares, or guards, who received us with civility. Mr. F.— was known to them, and one even embraced him, by saluting his forehead and calling him his intimate friend "ἀκριβέστατον φίλον". We were then announced to the Vizier, and immediately after admitted.

   The first approach to this extraordinary old man, whom I had so long desired to behold, was very interesting for me. The apartment in which we found the Vizier was of middling dimensions, but very lofty, and richly decorated in the Turkish style, without being overcharged.

14. Albanian official drawn by Otto Magnus von Stackelberg, 1811. The Gennadius Library, Athens.

The ceiling oval, or rather inclined in the elliptic form, was painted in deep celestial blue, with a number of stars in relief, gilt and of various sizes. This embellishment, which I had often seen in Turkish rooms at Constantinople, and elsewhere, seems to me to produce a very harmonious effect, especially in large apartments, which at the same time are rich in arabesques; but a similar decoration has appeared to me by far too striking and effective in small rooms, where it cannot harmonize with the rest. The saloon was oblong, and divided into two equal parts, by four light spiral columns, which rose from the floor to the ceiling. They were painted, like the ceiling itself, in sky blue, and intertwined with gilt foliage in relief, which united at the oblong chapiters in the large leaves of the acanthus, gilt, also, and in good taste. These columns with a gilded grating, separated the lower half of the apartment from the other part, which was elevated two steps, and occupied on three sides by a large Divan. This last was covered with red velvet curtains, elegantly attached to the tapestry by crescents in metal gilt and richly embellished with fringe and tafts of gold thread.

The Vizier was seated near a window, in the corner of the divan and cross legged (accroupi) upon a cushion rather larger than the rest. To the left, and a few paces from him on the divan and in the same posture, sat an elderly Turk, apparently an officer of high rank, a good looking man, with a much graver countenance than that of the Vizier. Lower down and upon the variegated carpet on the floor, that is the space surrounded by the divan, were three secretaries or transcribers, two of whom, Greeks, were before the Vizier, the third an Albanian, at least dressed as such, nearer the Turk just named; all the three were cross-legged, and employed in writing, their inkstand before them, under the dictation of the Vizier himself and the Ottoman officer. They all wrote without otherwise supporting the paper, than upon their left hand or upon their knee. I have often admired the neatness and rapidity, with which the Greeks and Turks thus wrote, but accustomed to the support of a desk or table, I have never been able to succeed in that manner.

As we approached the Divan the Vizier saluted us in the Turkish fashion — bowing the head, and bringing the right hand to the breast. He then made us a sign to sit down upon the Divan, not far from himself. On some words, spoken to the secretaries, they directly withdraw. There remained but the old Turk, who was the mute personage of the scene I am about to describe. The officer of the Tzucadores, who had introduced us, kept his station at the door at the other extremity of the apartment. The Vizier knew that he had no need of another interpreter when Mr. F.— was present; and I in my turn had requested the latter to let me try whether I could converse with the Pacha without intermediate aid. In his concise and lively manner, and in Greek, which he spoke commonly and the best, Ali asked me my name, my country, what was the object of my travels, if I had ever been in Greece before, if I was pleased with these countries, if I had been in them a long time...?

He put so many questions to me in a breath, that I hardly knew which to reply to first. I told him my name, my country, and that I had already been two or three years in Greece, travelling especially περιέργειας χάριν to see its ancient monuments etc. I added, moreover, I admit it, that I came at present to view the ancient Epirus, and to present my respects to His Highness, who was frequently spoken of in our parts of the world. On hearing those words he turned, with a smile, a little deceitful, to Mr. F.– and said — "I perceive this stranger has been long enough in these countries to have acquired the art of compliment-ing in *romaika* (vulgar Greek)" He accompanied this expression with a burst of laughter, so overpowering, that he almost deafened me this first time.

This immoderate laughter recurred often, it was one of his singu-larities, and never did I hear any other man laugh in such a manner. Turning again towards me, he said. "I like to converse with you with-out an interpreter. If you are come here to see me, I hope you will per-ceive, that I am not quite so bad as they describe me in the French newspapers" — another burst of laughter.

The Vizier was smoking tobacco when we entered, for which pur-pose he, generally, used that kind of machine which the Turks call *Arguilè*, where the smoke passed through the water which is deposited in a globe, or cylinder, mounted upon a large silver or bronze stand, frequently handsomely worked in filligree. A few paces from Ali Pacha, upon the carpet, was a similar instrument, from whence issued a morocco tube, long, elastic and intertwined with threads of gold which terminated in a *bouguet* of amber, very handsomely adorned with dia-monds, which the Vizier held in his hand. The dress of Ali offered but two things remarkable, which at once struck the sight; those were, a dagger he wore in his girdle, the handle of which was covered with diamonds, and a kind of cap, or rather of high calotte, of violet velvet, with large gold lace. The exact form of this calotte may be seen on his portrait of astonishing resemblance, drawn by Mr. Dupré (hh).[18] It bears some slight resemblance to the cap which the ancients gave to the figure of Ulysses (h.h.h.).[19]

Ali was rather below the middling stature. His head struck me as very remarkable, not the least like that of an Albanian, neither in shape or complexion, both of which appeared to me completely Greecian. The forehead was high and broad, the eyes of moderate size and without any decided colour, but extremely animated; the nose large and aquiline, the cheeks wide and full without being fleshy; the chin copious, round and covered with a white beard, which was not then so bushy as six years after, when Mr. Dupré made his fine drawing, from which I have had an engraving executed for this work. The most interesting, and most characteristick, expression in his face proceeded from his eyes, or rather from his look; and from that part which surrounds the mouth and the lips. His frequent smile had, usually, nothing of deceit or cunning, but often of much graciousness; and when animated by conversation, a gay and jovial air, truly agreeable, spread itself over his features. In general this wonderful man seemed to me, by his physiognomy, and by his manners, to assimilate as little with an old Turk of high rank as it is possible to imagine. He had nothing of that white and delicate complexion, which is so common amongst the Turkish seigniors; his own was brown and manly; his manners, concise and lively, had absolutely none of that slowness and gravity, which is the *bon ton* with the Turks of high rank. Ali, as the Greeks told me, even frequently mocked such a theatrical sort of gravity. He spoke quick, moved with rapidity, and in one word, had nothing of an old Turk, except his dress; — his body was that of a Greek, and his soul that of an Albanian.

These personal qualities must, necessarily, have had an influence upon the Turks themselves, established in Albania. In fact, those stubborn and haughty beings appeared less supine, and more tractable in Albania, than in any of the other Turkish provinces; because they there found themselves placed more upon a level with the other race of men, the Greeks and Albanians; — for Ali was too supremely despotic to value or favour any person whoever he was, othervise than by reason of his merit, that is — by his capacity to serve him in executing his schemes, good or bad. If it be true, as the immortal Aratus observes, (i)[20], that most princes, with indifference and egotism at the bottom of their hearts, only estimate in the individual, even the most noble, the means he possesses to be useful to them; and that their friendship, their contempt, and their hatred are solely decided by this calculation; could it then have been exacted of an Albanian despot, a man of genius, but uncultivated, to have a heart less dry, and sentiments less selfish?

15. Ali Pasha, drawn by L. Dupré, 1819. The Gennadius Library, Athens.

Ali had made a sign to the officer of his guards who was at the door, to let us have coffee and pipes. The Albanian, who served the sweet-meats and the coffee upon a large salver of silver, bent one knee to the ground in presenting them, first to the Vizier, next to us. Ali again asked me if I had not said that I was Danish. I answered in the affirmative. "It seems to me" rejoined he, that you are at arms length, your people, with the English these last years." (He used the following expression: μοῦ φαίνεται ὅτι εἴστε πλακισμένοι μὲ τοὺς Ἰγγλέσους ἐτούτους τοὺς χρονούς) and that I have read something about it in the Gazette of Corfu?" At this question, which Mr. F.— and myself would gladly have evaded, we looked at each other and smiled. I replied that some differences had, doubtless, existed between the two governments, but it was to be hoped they would soon be adjusted.

"Well", said he, "things change often, yonder, in your countries, and *friendships shift about this way and that way."*

He uttered these words in so pleasant a manner, it emboldened me to reply "Yes, your highness, much about the same as here in Turkey." Here he renewed his violent burst of laughter, and said: "It is true — it is true" (ἀλήθεια λέγεις, ἀλήθεια λέγεις) repeating several times these words.

His discontinued the subject, and I was very glad of it. He next put several questions to me, relative to my country, its population, its government etc. Two things struck him in my replies, first — that Denmark in the time of its prosperity (alas!) had possessed a fleet of twenty-two ships of the line, and fourteen or fifteen frigates; secondly — that the interesting country of Norway, which had not yet been separated from the Danish monarchy, extended so high up in the north. He had heard something of Iceland, especially of the volcano of Hecla, but was not aware that this island belonged to Denmark, having believed it to be a dependency on England. He inquired if it was true, as some travellers had told him, that the volcano of Hecla had a communication with that of Etna in Sicily, so that their eruptions often took place at the same time.

I answered that, according to all appearance, the great volcanick forges of our globe had much physical intelligence with each other, but that, however, was no reason why the eruption of one volcano should not be entirely local and that if the two of which he spoke, had had simultaneous eruptions it was, probably, an accidental coincidence.

"I have always wished," replied he, "to see a volcano, though not yours, up there at the extremity of the north, it is too cold there; but that of Etna or Vesuvius. The climate must needs be fine in Sicily and in a part of Italy, but, on the other hand, they have their inconveniences. — They tell me there are robbers on the high roads younder in Italy."

"I encountered none of those," replied I, but unfortunately, I have met with some here in Turkey." — "In what part?" "Upon the chain of mountains of Pentedactylon (Taygetus) in going from Mistra to Calamatha in the Morea, not far from the frontiers of Mayna".

I then related to him something of my rencounter with the robbers, who had entirely plundered me and my people, a few month before. He laughed much at my having arrived almost naked, and with but four *paras* in my pocket, at Calamatha; and inquired how I had received a fresh supply of money etc.

He next said, — "when you part from hence I will give you a passport (bouglourdi), and one of my people to attend you; we shall then see whether you are able to find me a single robber in all Albania — what say you of it Mr. F.—?"

The latter said some flattering words on the security of travelling through the whole extent of his states etc. For myself I could not help thinking that I knew *one* robber in his territories, and the greatest of them all, but, of course, I kept this to myself. He then talked with me of my travels in Turkey, of Constantinople, of Troias, of Smyrna, and above all, of Athens, a city which he told me he much desired to see.

In speaking of the ancient monuments of Athens, Mr. F.— observed, by mere accident, that my friends and myself had made several excavations in different parts of Greece, and that, some months previous, I had assisted at a great undertaking of that kind in Arcadia, in the Morea (this was the excavation of the temple of Apollo Epicurius of Phigalia). These words which Mr. F.— had spoken inconsiderately, and with no other intention than to talk of something or other, became in some sort fatal to me; as they occasioned me a delay of five days at Prevesa. I was, however, amply repaid for the loss of time by the advantage which it afforded me of seeing Ali Pacha, under circumstances new, and even *piquants*. The Vizier, at once seizing the words of Mr. F.—, eagerly demanded if I had been one of those *Mylords*, who had lately given a large sum of money to his son Vely Pacha of the Morea for permission to excavate somewhere? I told him that my friends, two Englishmen and two Germans, had undertaken that interesting excavation, at which I was present, and related to him something of the manner in which it was performed; the number of workmen employed upon it; the result of the operation etc.

He seemed, particularly, to interest himself in the part, which his son Vely had taken in the matter, and in the *money* which it had cost; and, all at once, said to me — "Well I see that you must be well skilled in *old stones*; I am glad of it. My son wrote to me of the marbles found in the Morea; I myself, also have *old stones* in this country. I have, moreover, a good many (he laughed much in uttering this), and if you have a mind to excavate some part in Albania, I will furnish you with as many people as you wish for nothing; — but it is to be understood that I will have my share of the marbles, and *precious things* (ἀπὸ τὰ τίμια πράγματα) that we find. What say you to this proposal?"

Although all this was said in a sportive tone, I felt notwithstanding, that his intention was serious enough, and I declined, in my best manner, to undertake excavations against my own will, by saying that I had, already, been six or seven years absent from my native country, and that I was actually obliged, by my connexions, to accelerate my voyage, by Corfu, Italy and Germany to Denmark etc. I, therefore, intreated His Highness to excuse me.

"You have, nevertheless, sufficient time," retorted the Pacha (and I clearly saw that he was a little vexed at the difficulties I had started) to go with me to the ruins of Nicopolis; they are not more than a league from hence."

Seeing the opportunity to soften the effect of my previous refusal, I answered that I should be entirely at His Highness's commands for that purpose, if it pleased him to fix the following day, or the day after, for our little excursion.

"It shall be tomorrow, if you please, and you Mr. F.—" turning towards him, " must be of the party; — I will send somebody to you this evening, to arrange the affair."

A Tartar having been announced a few minutes before, I availed myself of the occasion to take leave. The Pacha again said that he had felt much pleasure in conversing with me, and that the next day we would go to Nicopolis — καὶ αὔριον πᾶμεν εἰς τὴν Νικόπολιν, εἰς τὴν Νικόπολιν —.

He saluted us, in an affectionate manner, and Mr. F.— and myself retired.

My first visit to Ali Pacha had much amused me, but the excursion for the next day was not to my taste. I consulted Mr. F.— to ascertain if there were any method to evade it, but he strongly dissuaded me from any attempt of that kind. I was, therefore, bound to submit. In the interim behold, all at once, our learned *pachalique* excursion to the ruins of Nicopolis suspended!

The vizier had received in the afternoon some new visitors, foreign gentlemen, and also foreign ladies. The English Colonel M.C. and Major A.—,[21] in the British service, had arrived in the evening from St. Maure (where I had the advantage of making their aquaintance). They were accompanied by the Colonel's wife, his daughter, a pretty little child, and a Mrs. E.—,[22] the wife of an English officer at Zante, and the friend of the Colonel's lady. The gentlemen were come to purchase corn of the Vizier, for the use of the Ionian Isles, and the ladies had profitted of so favourable an opportunity for seeing a Turkish town, and the famous Ali Pacha. If the Vizier, his retinue, and the town, were objects of curiousity to these ladies, assuredly they themselves, in their turn, were not less so to the good folks of Prevesa. Indeed it was natural enough that the Vizier's officers — who came with him from the most remote parts of Albania. and were only accustomed to see respectable women promenade veiled, and with much circumspec-tion, — should be greatly astonished to behold these ladies, one of whom was very young and handsome, walking every where, with us gentlemen, unveiled, and with that air of freedom, which the more simple, and unconstrained manners of our countries permit.

The astonishment of the officers of the Tzucadares, and of the other Albanians, increased, in proportion with the marks of attention, shown to the ladies, and to us, by the Vizier; as the latter, who had apparently made a good bargain with the English gentlemen, evinced himself from the first exceedingly polite to the females, which, naturally, must have produced its effect upon all his slaves. He had given apartments to this interesting party, in one of the pavilions of his new palace, and placed a detachment of his guard at their orders. They were scarcely settled there, when the Pacha, who occupied the palace in the other quarter of the town, sent to them to announce his intention of paying a visit to the ladies. Half an hour after he came in his carriage, dressed in the Turkish costume, and with a sort of attendant pomp. I was present at this visit and, occasionally, acted as interpreter, for the Vizier's Greek Dragoman, being totally unacquainted with the English language, could only communicate with the ladies in Italian, a language which they themselves were not too well acquainted with, — and I can affirm that Ali, in every respect, comported himself, and entertained his company, with a politeness, and dignity, which struck us all. He offered his carriage to the female part of the company, and his saddle horses to us, to make an excursion in the afternoon to Nicopolis; then, turning towards me, said — "As for you and I, we will go together afterwards; we are agreed on that point are we not?" I, of course, answered in the affirmative.

He also invited the ladies to sup with him in his Harem in the evening, after their return from the ruins, apologizing in a graceful manner, at not being able to promise them a numerous society (he had brought but four of his women with him), nor very handsome apartments; as the building of the Harem at Prevesa was not yet completed. He then said to me, in Greek, that he regretted he could not engage us gentlemen to be of the party, owing to the Turkish customs which we must be acquainted with.

During the whole of this interview, his violent burst of laughter escaped him but once — on the following account. He had made the Dragoman ask the Colonel whether he would permit his wife to go with the Vizier in the evening to see the Harem. I paid no attention to the reply of the Colonel himself, but I accurately heard the interpreter's translation of it — "that the Colonel had nothing to say against the Vizier's proposal, and that he was fully persuaded his wife could not be better off, than in the society of His Highness." — at these words, very proper moreover, he gave way, I know not why, to his odd kind of laugh. Some pecuniary business prevented my joining in the afternoon excursion to Nicopolis.

The next day I found the ladies quite delighted with their evening's entertainment at the Harem. They highly extolled the grace and elegant manners of some of the Vizier's women, as well as their politeness to them. The Vizier came to breakfast, and, as on the preceeding day, was very obliging and very gay. He invited us all to pass the evening at the other palace inhabited by himself.

He arrived there at sunset. Colonel M.C. had brought with him three or four of the hautboys of his regiment; and, after refreshments had been served, he asked — whether his Highness would permit them to execute some marches, and other military music. The Vizier was much amused with them. When the musicians had performed some pieces, the Pacha said, that above all things he should feel greatly obliged to the ladies, and to us all, if we would show him some specimens of the dances of our countries, which he knew nothing of and much desired to see. The ladies made no objection whatever. We were but eight persons, amongst whom were only three females, but in travelling such matters are soon arranged, especially under similar circumstances. A waltz was readily formed, with very good music; then a species of french contredanse, followed by a scotch. The ladies danced very well, but the Colonel's little girl, a pretty child not more than ten years old, particularly and highly amused our aged spectator, who at times laughed with all his might. In other respects the Vizier was wrong in admiring these ordinary dances of society, which are either monotonous and languid, or, like most inventions of art in the time of Louis 14, full of affectation and pretension. He had still less reason to praise those unmeaning rotations, as he must have been accustomed to something of the kind infinitely superior, — that is — the national dance of the Albanians, which is one of the prettiest I ever saw. By its sentimental expression it approaches to the Spanish fandango, and by its rapid and difficult movements to the superb Norwegian national dance called *Halling*. I have seen the Albanian dance executed singly and in couples. The soldiers in dancing it retain their arms (except the musket) and then, chiefly, it seems literally to resemble the ancient military dance of the Epiriotes, often mentioned by old authors, and named πυρρίχα (k).[23]

The English officers having terminated their business with the Pacha, were to embark, with their companies etc., for St. Maure, at an early hour the ensuing day; they accordingly took leave of Ali this same evening. In bidding adieu to the ladies, he presented a pair of diamond earrings to the Colonel's wife, a diamond scorpion pin to Mrs. E.—, and a little ring with a solitaire to Miss M.C. He made these presents with much grace, and rose from the Divan (a rare instance of politeness in a Turk of high rank) in wishing them a good voyage, and in repeating — that it would be much more in his power to amuse the ladies, if they would one day make him a visit at his residence at Joanina. They were enchanted, as they had reason to be, with the politeness of

1810. 28. Aug.

16 (above), 17 (facing page). View of the ruins of Nicopolis. Drawing by Carl Haller von Hallerstein, August, 28th, 1811. Bibliothèque Nationale et Universitaire de Strasbourg.

Ali Pacha and when, in the evening as I accompanied them to the other palace, I asked Mrs. E.— what she thought of the Vizier — she answered me "I assure you I look upon him indeed, as the most amiable gentleman I ever saw." — I took the liberty of observing this praise of the Pacha was by no means a compliment for the rest of us.

The Vizier being busy the next day, the scientific excursion he had projected to Nicopolis did not take place; but he sent to inform Mr. F.— and myself, that he had fixed the following day for that purpose, and at the same time to inquire whether we would go with him in his carriage or rather chose to go on horseback. I preferred the latter as we should then be more at our ease.

At the time appointed we presented ourselves at the palace. The Vizier appeared to be in *Kiéfi*, as the Turks call it, that is in good humour; he directly entered his carriage, and we mounted two very fine horses that were ready saddled for us. A hundred Tzucadares escorted the Vizier's carriage, some on horseback, but the greatest part on foot.

Nicopolis *fait y' tage Paleocastro.*

Mr. F.— and myself now put our superb coursers in motion, unfortunately, however, they had the common fault of Turkish steeds, they could neither trot, nor pace, but kept constantly at a full or hand gallop; which was still more inconvenient for us, the road being intolerably bad, and the Vizier's carriage, in consequense, advancing very slowly. He repeatedly addressed a few words to us from the coach window, which on one of these occasions, led to an incident of a serio-comic nature.

The officers on horseback who surrounded his carriage, wishing to make way for me to answer some question of the Vizier, two of the horses slipped from the edge of the miry road into a pretty large ditch; one of them fell and the rider, an officer richly drest, was completely covered with dirt; furious at this accident, he avenged himself on the poor animal, but durst not return to the town. When the Pacha saw him in this state, at Nicopolis, he laughed heartily at his mishap, telling him — that, in his present plight he bore a great resemblance to one of those antique idols we were going to dig for.

Arrived at the ruins we alighted near one of those shepherds or goatherds huts, many of which are scattered over the vast extent of ground covered by the dilapidated walls and buildings of the ancient city. The Vizier entered the hut, where they had prepared for him a carpet, some cushions, a service of coffee, and his *arguilé*, with pipes for us. He invited Mr. F.— and myself to sit down on the cushion near to him; the others remained abroad, where they made some excellent coffee. In waiting for it, the Pacha conversed with the poor peasant who occupied the hut, of his flocks, his family etc. The good man seemed to be quite enlivened, and very much pleased and talked with the Vizier, without the least reserve. His dialect was a provincial Greek, mixed with the Albanian.

While we were taking coffee, and smoking, the Vizier begged me to give him some account of the ancient city of Nicopolis, its population, and its fate. When I had related as much as I could recollect of the principal events connnected with the interesting locality, he told me that he had already been acquainted with every thing I had just stated; and had merely questioned me on the subject, to compare my account with that which an Englishman had given him, some time before, of the history of Nicopolis. He said that our statements perfectly accorded, and expressed much surprise (a thing which often happens to us with the Turks) — that we Franks, at the extremity of the world, should be so well aquainted with their countries, and their cities. The Pacha then rose, requesting me to go out with him — *to show him something handsome* (νὰ μοῦ δείξῃς εὔμορφόν τι) as he termed it. I shook my head a little at this request, observing that, probably, I should not be able to show his Highness any thing, but what he had already seen much oftener than me. "It is well," retorted he, but you are a connoisseur, your eyes are better than mine, "καλήτερα μάτια ἔχεις, καλήτερα μάτια" and he laughed as he said this. We first proceeded to the great square of walls nearest to us. This great square, of the time of Augustus, of a very fine and strong masonry, is in the enclosure of the ancient city. The Pacha demanded my opinion on the object of these fortifications. I answered that I considered them as the enclosure of the residence of the Roman Emperors, when they came, sometimes, to Nicopolis; I added that, according to my opinion, this had been the *arx*, or fortified building, destined to contain a guard-house, barracks, magazines of arms etc.; in short that this immense square had been to the city of Nicopolis, built in a plain, that which the *Acropolis* were in the Greek cities, situated upon or contiguous to mountains. The Vizier admired the fine masonry, spoke, not without intelligence, of the Roman method of building, and inquired if we had yet, in our countries, artisans who knew how to make such bricks, and to prepare a cement so strong and binding? We next came to the small theatre, from whence there is a fine view over almost all the ruins of the ancient city. He asked me some reminiscenses of the great theatre, that we saw at a certain distance: he had entertained the erroneous idea that it had been a kind of camp or rather a fortified guard-house. Our ensuing topic was the *stade*, which was also before us, and near the great theatre. What I related of the origin, and destination, of the stade appeared to be new to him; he assured me he should be disposed to have its inner space smoothed for his Albanians to practice there the races, as in former days, "but", added he, "my people are light enough and agile enough without that" — (in which he was certainly quite correct for there hardly exists a race of men in Europe more nimble than the Albanians) — "when I was young", continued he, "I was as fleet as a hind, but at present I am old and too corpulent".

He now requested me to show him some places, where we might dig for ancient marbles and other curiosities. The *we* was pronounced with a certain emphasis, notwithstanding my protestations made some days before on the subject, and I began to fear that he had a relapse of the sort. I therefore repeated to him, what I had already said, that I did not believe excavations made at Nicopolis, would even produce results of any importance in point of sculpture; since it was sufficiently proved, by history, that this great city had been plundered of its best monuments by Constantine the Great, and subsequently sacked by Alarick. I added that I would show, however, to His Highness two ruins in the interior of the the city, which had evidently been temples, and where, perhaps, some fragments might be found, in digging carefully. We proceeded to one of those ruins, and the Pacha, being pleased with the locality, made a sign to one of his Tzucadares, who went out calling some Albanian words in a loud voice, and instantaneously about twenty peasants hastened from one of the huts, furnished with mattocks, shovels, axes etc. Having known nothing of these preparations, I began seriously to be afraid, that I was about to become *an Excavator in spite of myself*. My apprehensions on this subject increased, when the Vizier made them bring the cushions and his pipe from the hut where we had breakfasted. From all this it seemed as if he was disposed to take up his quarters on the spot.

The ruin, in which we stood, had been a rectangular edifice, very

Vorgebirge von Actium

1810. 28. Aug.

18. Nicopolis. View from the great theatre towards the Island of Leukas (Sa. Maura). Drawing by Carl Haller von Hallerstein, August, 28th, 1811. Bibliothèque Nationale et Universitaire de Strasbourg.

likely a temple, but without a peristyle; it appeared to me that the altar, or place of worship, at one of the extremities, had been elevated some steps upon the pavement from the rest of the building, as for example, it is seen in two small temples at Pompeii. Although the whole was nearly on the same level owing to the rubbish of the entablature, the greater part of which had fallen into the interior of the edifice. On three sides of the walls were niches regularly disposed.

Obliged, as I was, to assist at this odd kind of excavation, and being neither able nor willing to proceed in order, I proposed, at least, to

Insul St. Maura -

Rückseite des großen Theaters von Nicopolis.

clear away the earth under two of the niches on the long side of the
building, which the Pacha approved of. His people set themselves
stoutly to work, which became however, very laborious, as I had fore-
seen, from the want of necessary implements; especially of iron levers,
indispensable to move the large stones fallen from the entablature; the
strong ropes, besides, to draw out the other masses, which incom-
moded the workmen; and finally, the large baskets, to take away the
earth. I observed to the Vizier that all this was nearly labour lost, without the proper tools. He comprehended it, and gave orders that every-
thing requisite should be brought the next day, and a shed constructed
to hold the implements, and the things we were going to find. In the
mean time they continued, for better for worse, to dig amongst the rubbish in two places. At the expiration of an hour in penetrating, by one

of these excavations, to the soil, three fine square marble slabs were found, probably part of the ancient pavement of the building. The Vizier had them placed, with the greatest care upon a sort of rolling/sedan-chair (chaise roulante) and covered with straw, to be conveyed to Prevesa. In the other cavity were found two insignificant bronze medals, in tolerable good preservation, both of them of Nicopolis; the one struck under Commodus, the other under Caracalla. The Vizier gave me the last, and pocketed the other himself, laughing at this *augmentation of his treasury*.

The Pacha's pipe being out, he, at length, rose, apparently much satisfied with his excavation. I partook in his satisfaction, but from a different cause. He gave some money to the poor peasant, who in the morning had received us in his hut, we did the same, and then mounted, he in his carriage, we on our inconvenient steeds to return to Prevesa. We went on before, and received the old seignior on foot on his arrival at the palace, according to the etiquette of this noble court Pachalique. I availed myself of some pretext to retire, which the Pacha, at last, permitted me to do, and, also, appointed me the hour for my final interview at the palace the day following.

At eleven o'clock in the forenoon I went with Mr. F.— to the palace, conformable to the Vizier's invitation; having arranged for my departure the same day.

I found there a number of mountaineers, from the northern districts of Albania, of a physiognomy entirely Albanian, but of a complexion less dark, or livid, than those I had hitherto seen. We were told, in the antichamber, that these people were come by the Vizier's orders, in consequence of some disturbances which had taken place in their districts. Two villages had been disputing together, the others took part in contention, and from quarreling they proceeded to fighting; on hearing of which the Vizier was displeased etc. We were announced and immediately introduced.

The Vizier was in a handsome apartment, which I now beheld for the first time. It was one of his singularities never to occupy the same room two days together. Ali and one of his ministers were seated upon the Divan; a Greek secretary was upon its estrade, or raised floor, and at the extremity of this, in the other half of the room, two steps lower than the Divan, were kneeling fifteen of the mountaineers I just mentioned. The Vizier appeared to speak without passion to these poor people. I heard him laugh at the moment we were entering. He made me a sign to sit down on the Divan, and laughingly said: "I have had a proof of the truth you told me the other day, that they quarrel quite as well in Turkey as they do in your part of the world; these mountaineers have been disputing and came to blows; I must make myself the arbitrator between them". He made a movement with his hand and, the sign being understood, the peasants immediately withdrew to the antichamber. He ordered pipes and coffee to be brought in. At first he spoke of his Nicopolis; next of a quantity of great ruins, in the northern provinces of Albania, of which I knew nothing, and where we should, doubtless, find magnificent things, if I would remain with him some six or seven months etc. I offered the first excuse that occurred to me, but assured him, that if I came again to Turkey, I would not fail to present my homage to His Highness, and to avail myself, when circumstances permitted, of his gracious offer. He then asked me what was the plan of my travels. I told him that I had decided to go by land to Arta, and afterwards to pass by Pentepigadia, and the adjacent parts of the mountains of Suly, to Joanina etc. He interrupted me saying " If you had taken that route ten years ago you would have been robbed" (this was in reference to the state of those parts before Suly had been subjugated); "you may now proceed to Arta, and to Joanina, as tranquilly as we went yesterday to Nicopolis. I will give you a *Bouglourdi*, and one of my people, and you will write me from Joanina, or from Sajades, whether you have been satisfied with him and if my residence has pleased you".

He ordered one of his guards to be called, (Dimo of Argyrocastro, the young man before spoken of) and commanded him to conduct me in a proper manner; to do what I required of him; and to take special care not to bring a bad certificate from me on his return. He ordered him, besides, to be sure to see that every thing was opened to my inspection in the seraglio, and the Vizier's other pleasure-houses at Joanina; after which he dictated to his secretary my Bouglourdi. In signing it, and giving it to me, he persuaded me much to go to Argyrocastro, to see his youngest and favourite son *Suli Bey*, a youth then about twelve or thirteen years old, and who was educating there, by his orders, — far from the court and the intrigues of Joanina. He had, undoubtedly, formed great projects in regard to this fine child, but providence has since otherwise disposed of his days, and those of his

19. The Palace and the Fortress of Ali Pasha in Ioannina, drawn by L. Dupré. The Gennadius Library, Athens.

children. He gave me, also, a commission for his man of business, a Greek, at Venice, of which he had already spoken to me, at our first interview. It related to seventy six looking-glasses of various sizes, for the decoration of some of his seraglios. — I subsequently fulfilled this commission at Venice. When I took leave of him, he entreated me, in a manner truly affectionate, and amiable, to write to him sometimes, but, above all, to return soon to remain a long time, that we might excavate together in the northern districts of Albania. He rose in bidding me farewell: "νὰ πάῃς καλὰ, ὁ Θεὸς νὰ σε φιλάξῃ, νὰ εὑρίσκῃς πάντα καλὰ εἰς τὸν τόπον σου, καὶ νὰ γυρίσῃς ὀγλίγωρα—!": A good voyage, a happy voyage, god protect you, may you find every happiness in your own country, and come back soon!" — I still heard at the door these words reiterated "νὰ γυρίσῃς ὀγλίγωρα! εἰς τὸ καλό!" — "come back soon, happy voyage!"

I own that this extraordinary man made a great impression upon me. Others have seen him under a point of view wholly different; I saw him, absolutely, as I have represented him here. The difference is in the nature of things. Ali was one of those volcanos of a *hundred aspects*, which providence makes use of in its moral administration as in the physical world, to execute its designs. But these volcanos do not always throw out torrents of fire, and I know of delightful gardens on the sides of Etna, and of Vesuvius, which each year put on the finest verdure, close to those horrible heaps, which have borne on their burning waves death and destruction.[24]

20. Nicopolis. Part of a wall, called "εις το ριζαμ". Drawn by Carl Haller von Hallerstein August 28th, 1811. Bibliothèque Nationale et Universitaire de Strasbourg.

Appendix
On Nicopolis
(from Brøndsted, *Reise i Grækenland* I, 235-36)

Since much has been written about the ruins of Nicopolis in the last century, I shall be brief about this other large Epirotic city at the Gulf, the youngest of them all in antiquity. Thanks to their geographical position these ruins were easily accessible to the traveller, who, having no intention of investigating the inner parts of Greece, was visiting only the dependencies of Venice on these coasts, among them Prevesa and its nearest surroundings.

The ruins of Nicopolis are situated on a rather low tongue of land, created by the Gulf, east of Prevesa about half a mile [3.5 km] from this city. Augustus had placed most part of this, his favourite town, on this lower isthmus or tongue of land, but in such way, that the whole construction forms an extensive oblong square or rather a rectangle which also includes part of the spurs from the mountain, that limits the northern horizon of Prevesa and Nicopolis. Especially from this higher area there is a very fine view on the one side of Actium, the gulf, and the coast of Acharnania and on the other side of the Ionian Sea in the West. The extensive ruins are all made of bricks, but of very high quality workmanship. But, in the field of architecture Nicopolis does not contribute with anything new to our knowledge of Roman constructions, known to us from so many ruins in Rome and elsewhere.[25] This is also the opinion of Baron Haller, my friend and travelling companion. The walls of the *arx Imperatoris* or the Imperial fortress of Augustus are still preserved. Of the other notable public buildings, one very large theatre, a smaller one, and a stadium are among the best preserved. The larger theatre, which is built into the forementioned higher area in the north, offers a very interesting spot, from which one has a beautiful view of the extensive constructions of the ancient city, which, certainly, is made in a higher more grandiose style.

21. [Top] Other part of the wall. [Bottom] Plan of the terrace. Paleo-Castro = Nicopolis. Drawing by Carl Haller von Hallerstein, August 28th, 1811. Bibliothèque Nationale et Universitaire de Strasbourg.

This in combination with the small huts of the shepherds, which here and there join the huge, ancient walls, and with the flocks of sheeps and goats, which usually graze among the ruins, creates a landscape, rich in features, with no lack of interesting and moving contrasts.

Augustus' vanity led him in part to attract in part to force a large quantity of the population of Acharnania and Epirus to leave their former homes and to settle in his City of Victory. First and foremost Leukas, Ambrakia, Thyrreum, Anaktorium, and Argos Amphilochium, which the latest revolutions in Greece had left almost empty, had to cede the rest of their inhabitants to the popular Nicopolis. (*Cf. Strabo, Pausanias, and Antipater in Bruncks *Analecta*. T. II. p. 117 [*Analecta vet. poetar. graecor.*, Strasb. Acad., 1785]). The city construction and its ruins give us evidence of a city, which might hold around 200,000 inhabitants. Nicopolis was declared a *civitas libera* and recieved privileges, which later Roman Emperors do not seem to have respected. The Emperor Julian found Nicopolis a decayed and poor city in 362 AD; and about forty years after the visit of this Emperor, in the reign of Arcadius, Nicopolis seems to have been utterly devastated by Alaric, who towards the end of the fourth century with his Visigoths traversed and raided the Peloponnesus and other parts of the Greek continent.

A large quantity of marble columns and other movable building materials from the ruins has been dragged away during these last years by orders from Ali Vizier to be used for the building of the two palaces of the Pacha and a couple of mosques in Prevesa, recently completed.

Notes

1. For instance in the works of Mr Bartholdy [Bruchstücke...Berlin, 1805], Dr. Clarke etc. This costume is also distinctly displayed in the engravings given in this work, after the fine drawing of Ali Pacha's hunting-barge by Mr. Dupré.

2. This custom of shaving the sinciput is very ancient with some of the tribes of Greece. Homer had already mentioned it, in speaking of the Abantes a people of the Island of Euboea. Iliad II, 542 τῷ δ᾽ ἅμ᾽ Ἄβαντες ἕποντο θοοί, ὄπιθεν κομόωντες αἰχμηταὶ κ.τ.λ. ["Him followed the nimble Abantes, warriors with hair only at the back (of the head)"] (Heyne, [C. G. Heyne in his edition of *Homeri Ilias*, 1802] was mistaken in saying — *Var. Lect.* and *observ. ad h. l.* - : "igitur occipite raso esse debuere" ["therefore it must be with the occiput shaven"], it was the contrary: "occipite comantes" ["with hair only on the occiput"]).

   Plutarch also relates in the beginning of his Life of Theseus that this hero had shaved the sinciput in honour of the Delphian God; from whence came the denomination ἡ Θησεία, by which the operation is designated. Plutarch cites in the same place the habit of the Abantes by saying they had adopted it, to prevent their enemies seizing them by the hair in battle: μὴ παρέχοιεν ἐκ τῶν τριχῶν ἀντίληψιν τοῖς πολεμίοις, and that Alexander the Great had commanded his soldiers to shave their long beards from the same reason. The custom to let the hair of the sinciput grow, was also in use with some tribes during the heroic times. It is thus that Homer [Iliad IV, 533] calls a people of Thracia Θρήϊκες ἀκρόκομοι ["top-knotted Thracians"].

3. See Colonel Martin Leake's Researches in Greece; Dr. Holland's Travels in Greece.

4. This was by order of the Roman senate, the execrable policy of which sometimes required that an army, which had conquered one country, should, as a reward, have permission to plunder another. The senate disposed of a whole nation in favour of its victorious soldiers, just as the shepherd may dispose of a lamb of his flock in favour of his dogs, who had killed the wolf. The senate had its political reasons — (and politicks as well that of the Romans as that of our days is, as all the world knows, a science most *human* and most *rational*) — to spare Macedonia after the defeat of its wretched and last king Perseus. They wished *at that time* to persuade the Macedonians that their hostility had been directed against *him* solely. But after a victory so signal, as that which Emilius gained near the river *Leucus*, — after the conquest of a great kingdom in two days, the Roman Army, of course, expected some recompense. Very well, said the senate to Paulus Aemilius: pass over with your army to Epirus, and there eat, drink, destroy, sack and sell as much as you please. Emilius did as they had permitted him to do much against his own inclination we must believe — παρὰ τὴν φύσιν, says Plutarch, ἐπιεικῆ καὶ χρηστὴν οὖσαν [*Aem. Paul.* XXX, 1] This good and loyal consul, who had given such wise counsel first to the dethroned and degraded monarch, afterwards to his young *commilitones*

[fellow soldiers, here: the officers] (vide his Life by Plutarch c. 21.[= XXVI-XXVII]) made use of a strategem to fall with his famished wolves upon the miserable province of Epirus, before they had taken the least precaution against such a calamity. *Seventy* towns were sacked, more than a hundred and fifty thousand persons were sold as slaves and the definitive result of so many horrors and crimes was — that each Roman soldier went away with *eleven drachms* in his pocket! Plutarch, in accurately relating these facts, adds that every-body shuddered of this result of a war which after the extermination of a whole people ended by only producing an individual division so worthless and so pitiful [XXIX, 5]: φρίξαι δὲ πάντας ἀνθρώπους τὸ τοῦ πολέμου τέλος, εἰς μικρὸν οὕτω τὸ καθ᾽ ἕκαστον λῆμμα καὶ κέρδος ἔθνους ὅλου κατακερματισθέντος. Compare Strabo l. VII c. 7: τῶν δ᾽ οὖν Ἠπειρωτῶν ἑβδομήκοντα πόλεις Πολύβιος φησιν ἀνατρέψαι Παῦλον τὸν Αἰμίλιον μετὰ τὴν Μακεδόνων καὶ Περσέως κατάλυσιν eh! ["Polybius says that Aemilius Paulus after his subjection of the Macedonians and Perseus destroyed seventy cities of the Epeirotes."]

5. See his "Researches in Greece", London 1814.

6. Ali Pasha was killed by order of the Sultan on February 5th, 1822 on the island in the Lake of Ioannina. His embalmed head was sent to Constantinople by Courchid Pasha, who led the siege of Ali's palace in Ioannina. On February 24th the head was put on exhibition, nailed to the Seraglio gates. For the many detailed versions of the siege and the death of Ali Pasha, see the Bibliography.

7. The Life of Paulus Emilius c. 19. Plutarch, besides, calls Avarice *the innate disease of princes*. I am not able to say whether he is in the right.

8. In their works.

9. Some interesting details of this battle, and of the occupation of Prevesa by Ali Pacha, will be found in the "Travels of M. Pouqueville through the Morea and Albania" etc. Vol. 3.

10. We have some interesting details upon the different wars of Ali Pacha against the Souliotes in the work of Mr. Eton (Survey of the Turkish Empire. London 1798 8° p. 371) and in that of Mr. Bartholdy (Bruchstücke etc. Berlin 1805 8° p. 478). No tribe of Modern Greece has been more distinguished, at once for their bravery and their misfortunes, or more given to plunder, than the Souliotes. In general the profession of freebooter, in the countries we are speaking of, does not at all exclude rare virtues; and to a great part of the provinces of Modern Greece may be applied with truth the remarks of Thucydides (Hist. book 1 chapt. 5) on the manner in which the Greeks were regarded in the heroic times: that this calling (of a robber) was by no means disgraceful, but, on the contrary, "creditable". I observe, besides, that Thucydides precisely quotes the example of the different tribes of that part of the continent, of which we speak here, who yet in his time led a life of liberty and of plunder; and that he regarded their custom of going always armed (a custom still, in the present day peculiar to the Albanians) as a habit they retained from their ancient profession: — οὐχ ἔχοντός πω αἰσχύνην τούτου τοῦ ἔργου (τῆς λῃστείας), φέροντος δέ τι καὶ δόξης μᾶλλον. δηλοῦσι δὲ τῶν τε ἠπειρωτῶν τινὲς ἔτι καὶ νῦν, οἷς κόσμος καλῶς τοῦτο δρᾶν, καὶ οἱ παλαιοὶ τῶν ποιητῶν τὰς πύστεις τῶν καταπλεόντων πανταχοῦ ὁμοίως ἐρωτώντως εἰ λῃσταί εἰσιν, ὡς οὔτε ὧν πυνθάνονται ἀπαξιούντων τὸ ἔργον, οἷς τε ἐπιμελὲς εἴη εἰδέναι οὐκ ὀνειδιζόντων.

ἐληζοντο δὲ καὶ κατ᾽ ἤπειρον ἀλλήλους. καὶ μέχρι τοῦδὲ πολλὰ τῆς Ἑλλάδος τῷ παλαιῷ τρόπῳ νέμεται περὶ τε Λοκροὺς τοὺς Ὀζόλας καὶ Αἰτωλοὺς καὶ Ακαρνᾶνας καὶ ταύτη ἤπειρον. τό τε σιδηροφορεῖσθαι τούτοις τοῖς ἠπειρώταις ἀπὸ τῆς παλαιᾶς λῃστείας εμμεμένηκε. ["At this time such a profession, so far from being regarded as disgraceful, was considered quite honorable. It is an attitude that can be illustrated even today by some of the inhabitants of the mainland among whom successful piracy is regarded as something to be proud of; and in the old poets, too, we find that the regular question always asked of those who arrive by sea is 'Are you pirates?' It is never assumed either that those who were so questioned would shrink from admitting the fact, or that those who were interested in finding out the fact would reproach them with it. The same system of armed robbery prevailed by land; and even up to the present day much of Hellas still follows the old way of life — among the Ozolian Locrians, for instance, and the Aetolians and the Acarnanians and the others who live on the mainland in this area. Among these people the custom of carrying arms still survives from the old days of robbery." Transl. by R. Warner.]

Later in the third and second ages before our era and at one of the most remarkable epochs of ancient Greece, that is of the Achaian league, an entire Greek state, the republic of the Ætolians, which was for some time very powerful, existed so to express it, but by plundering. The contests of these people with the Achaian league (so ably described by Polybius) their continual incursions into the Peloponnesus, and elsewhere, had absolutely the character of a war of daring partisans, ready to combat for or against whoever it was, provided they gained by it; and Polybius was in the right to consider this disposition as *organic* with that warlike race. For instance Polyb. Hist. 1. II chap. 45: Αἰτωλοὶ διὰ τὴν ἔμφυλον ἀδικίαν καὶ πλεονεξίαν ["The Aetolians, because of their natural, unrighteous greediness..."], Id. 1. IV chap. 3: Δορίμαχος — νέος ὢν καὶ πλήρης Αἰτωλικῆς ὁρμῆς καὶ πλεονεξίας ["Dorimachos, being young and full of Aetolian energy and greediness..."].

This profession of κλέπτης (robber) still, in the present day, although illegal, and strongly disapproved, as it ought to be, by the government, is not at all regarded in Greece — not even in the provinces most advanced in civilization, with that horror which is with us the effect of the sentiment that every individual proves to submit himself to an order of things which guarantees the security of his person and property, in other words — to submit to the *state*.

In Turkey, on the contrary, where this security *for persons of property* does not often exist in the very bosom of the state; where the lives of individuals too frequently become precarious and dependent on the good or bad dispositions of the Pachas, Turkish Vaivodes, and other petty tyrants, the necessity to seek security *out of the state* must inevitably lessen in the mind the horror of such an existence. It results from this that the denomination κλέπται *thieves, robbers* is often confounded in Greece with the idea of *fugitives, malcontents* who have been forced by the authorised plunderers *to take to the mountains*, as they term it, and in their turn to act the parts of plunderers unauthorized. It is easy to imagine that if the chiefs of their bands possess energy and courage, the life of such vagabonds, beneath a fine sky, and in a region where there are great chains of mountains, may be singularly animated and, in a certain manner, poetical. Accordingly we found that some of the best songs of the people, which are now sung in Greece, either for the bold and free sentiments which the words express, or for their animated and rapturous harmony, were of a kind which they call κλεφτικὸν, that is "the Banditti's air". In Greece they often propose to sing you a κλεφτικὸν as in former times they would have proposed to sing airs in the Lydian or Doric mode. [The following sentence is deleted by the author, as no specimens of songs are found in the manuscript:] Amongst the Greek songs which will be published in this work, will be found several specimens of the κλεφτικὰ of the Greeks of today.

11. 36 in number, according to Brøndsted, *Reise i Grækenland*, vol. I, p. 245.
12. March 15th, 1812.
13. Theotocki and count Securo according to Brøndsted, *Reise i Grækenland* I, p. 247.
14. "C'est bien un de mes voeux politiques de rendre ma carte de visite un jour chez Monseur le voleur de Tepelen." Quoted by Brøndsted, *Reise i Grækenland* I, p. 248.
15. For the young count Nicolo Lunzi, see introduction p. 21.
16. Spiridon Forresti, the English minister at Zakynthos.
17. Ludvig Holberg (1684-1754), a Danish writer, famous for his comedies and satiric writings.
18. See the Plates No. V and VI [= Pl. No. 13 in this edition].
19. See the Vignette Plate X [now lost].
20. *Polybius* Hist. l. II cap. 47 §186 (ed. Amstelod. 1670 in 8o: pag. 186) — τούς δὲ βασιλεῖς σαφῶς εἰδὼς (Aratus) φύσει μὲν οὐδένα νομίζοντας οὔτε ἔχθρον οὔτε φίλον, τοὺς δὲ τοῦ συμφέροντος ψήφοις ἀεὶ μετροῦντας τὰς ἔχθρας καὶ φιλίας, ἐξεβάλετο λαλεῖν πρὸς τὸν εἰρημένον βασιλέα (to Antigonus called Doson of Macedonia) ["(Aratus)...knowing that kings do not regard anyone as their enemy or friend but that they measure enmities and friendships by the standard of benefit, decided to speak to the aforesaid king (Antigonus Doson)"].
21. Colonel Mack-Combe and Major Arrata.
22. Mrs. Echworth.
23. See Hesychius (Alberti's edition in fol. Lugd. Batav. 1766) under the words πυρρίχας and πυρριχίζειν, where Alberti quotes in his notes, most of the passages in the ancient authors, where this military danse of the Epirotes is treated on.
24. In *Reise i Grækenland*, vol. I, p. 270, Brøndsted has added the following sentence to his conclusion: "Many a beautiful flower may thrive under despotism, but certainly none in a status of anarchy."
25. In a recent article ("The Stadium at Aphrodisias", *AJA* 102, 1998, p. 564, note 62) Katherine Welch suggests that the stadium at Nicopolis was conceived and planned in Rome. According to her, its construction technique is typical of Early Imperial Rome (the Tiberian phase of the Castra Praetoria) but unparalleled in other buildings at Nicopolis and anywhere else in Greece.

Index